PURELY ORIGINAL VERSE

by

J. GORDON COOGLER

With original reviews and biographical sketch

by

Claude Henry Neuffer

and

Rene LaBorde

Columbia, S. C.: Vogue Press, 1974

This book is dedicated to "the Sage of Cedar Creek,"
Pierre Fabian LaBorde,
whose annotated copy first made
us Cooglerites.

J. GORDON COOGLER: BARD OF THE CONGAREE

> Alas, for the South! Her books have grown fewer—
> She never was much given to literature.

Perhaps the most quoted couplet in American verse, these lines and other such Cooglerisms gave immortality to the bard of solemn absurdities. Especially this was assured when in 1917 in the New York *Evening Post,* H. L. Mencken introduced his "Sahara of the Bozarts" with that couplet and this beginning tribute: "In the lamented J. Gordon Coogler, author of these elegiac lines, there was the insight of a true poet. He was the last bard of Dixie, at least in the legitimate line."

Of all Mencken's *opera,* the "Sahara" is his most reprinted essay—having been included in his frequently re-issued book of *Prejudices* (1920) and in American literature textbooks of required reading for students during the past fifty years. As Mencken himself noted in 1949 in the introduction to this same essay included in *A Mencken Chrestomathy:* "It produced a ferocious reaction in the South, and I was belabored for months, and even years afterwards in a very extravagant manner." (Ironically, his "Violets in the Sahara" from the Baltimore *Sun*—sincerely praising Julia Peterkin, DuBose Heyward, the South Carolina Poetry Society, and other Southern writers—has never been reprinted or anthologized.)

But long before Mencken's tribute—in fact, over twenty years before—in the 1890's Coogler's verse had swum into the ken of other enthusiastic critics throughout the country and even in England.

Charles A. Dana, "an ardent Cooglerite," editorialized in the New York *Sun:* "He is bold enough to attempt flights heretofore unessayed and he writes verse as no other man has ever written. The country owes much to J. Gordon Coogler."

Henry W. Grady, president of Atlanta's Coogler fan club (first of many nationwide, even in Boston) opined as editor of Atlanta *Constitution:* "There must be something in the writings of a man who can attract attention and win applause when corn is thirty cents a bushel and potato bugs have become a burden."

Munsey's Magazine nominated him for American poet laureate. *Puck, Bookman, Literary Digest, Godey's Magazine, Chap Book,* Detroit *Free Press,* Denver *Times*—magazines and newspapers from London, England, to Portland, Oregon, titled him Bard of the Congaree, Palmetto Poet, Songbird of the Saluda, dulcet-voice singer of Dixie. Their glowing reviews Coogler included in his later editions (and so here do we) of his complete works.

Now, over seventy years since he hung up his harp, comes a Coogler revival. Devotees, seeking refuge from obscure odes and pornographic prose of our latest literati, have looked in vain for their own copies of *Purely Original Verse.* And the plea went out from a kindred spirit:

> When my soul has come to tire
>   Of today's too bedeviled bugler,
> Oh, to be soothed by the ingenuous Apollo's lyre
>   Of Simplicity's own J. Gordon Coogler.

Answering popular demand, we have prepared this photographic reprint of our prize paternal legacy: Pierre Fabian LaBorde's annotated 1897 edition of *Purely Original Verse* by J. Gordon Coogler. Originally set in type by the bard himself in his own little print shop, the book has open o's, reverse pagination in the preface, two-line fillers so as not to waste space at the bottom of a page, and other such taboos that the modern bookmaker would term unesthetic. In this reprint, all has been preserved, for—as his devotees insist—the book must be truly Coogler.

Our own revived interest in the bard came a few years ago when Sandlapper Press commissioned us to write about Coogler. With kind permission of that press, we here draw from that article which appeared in *South Carolina Illustrated,* Vol. I, No. 3 (August 1970).

Turning the pages of Coogler's scant little volume reveals

eternal verities that surely might explain the present Coogler revival.

The bearded young man of today chortles over the reverse problem of Coogler's clean-shaven youth:

> He can't understand why the beautiful girls
>> Should thus be so cruel and rash,
> Unless they believe that kisses are sweeter
>> From lips that bear a mustache.

The complexion-troubled teenager might well be persuaded to try a new skin lotion, TV-commercialed with this Coogler quatrain:

> On her beautiful face there are smiles of grace
>> That linger in beauty serene,
> And there are no pimples encircling her dimples
>> As ever, as yet, I have seen.

Concerning water pollution and whisky-by-the-drink, the bard made his choice even before there were such problems:

> May your life, like the rose of summer,
>> Be fresh, and remain in its bud.
> As I never was partial to whisky,
>> I'll toast you in Congaree mud.

When birdwatchers are forced indoors by inclement weather, there remains the pleasure of reading of the activities of their feathered friends:

> The robin, the jaybird, and the crow
> All make tracks in the beautiful snow.

The pious Establishment might well turn red in both its faces:

> Oh, thou old gray-haired deceiver,
> Thou expounder of sacred Writ,
> Doest thou not know that God in Heaven
> Despises the hypocrite?

There are even appropriate lines concerning today's fashions—titles like "More Care for the Neck Than the Intellect," or "The Dude," or even maybe a put-down of women's lib:

> Sweet girl, I like to see you look
>   The very best you can;
> But please do not try so soon
>   To imitate a man.
>
> You are not masculine or neuter,
>   Neither of those genders;
> Therefore I'd advise you to
>   Take off those suspenders.

With such pure poetry to attract new admirers, prospective Cooglerites would wish to know a bit about the bard and his rocket-rise to fame. J. Gordon Coogler was born December 3, 1865, in Doko—the old name for the little community of Blythewood, north of the then war-torn town of Columbia, South Carolina. Permitted to select his own Christian name, he tried several until at age fourteen, he chose John Brown Gordon, the Confederate general and Georgia statesman.

When his father died in 1880, J. Gordon began learning a trade. By 1885, working in the printing office of David Augustus Childs, he with his family (his mother and three sisters—Florence, Lily, and Nonie) moved to Columbia. His two older brothers were reputedly rather wild (perhaps inspirations for poems like "Dissipation" or "Destroy It Not") and left care of home, hearth, and family females to their serious, sensitive brother.

Early an apt rhymer, Coogler rapidly became known as a versifier. He was often called upon to write an occasional poem to accompany a gift or tribute a lady. Long before printed greeting cards, in his little printshop window at 1226 Lady Street, the sign read "Poems Written While You Wait"— maybe such as:

> I'd rather hear an earthquake
>   As it roars 'neath hill and valley,
> Than to hear those angry undertones
>   From the pouting lips of Sally.

Though sometimes even Coogler's muse failed, he never said "No" completely:

> Fair maid, 'tis a "little gay poem" you wish,
>> But you cannot get it tomorrow;
> But some sweet day I'll grant your request
>> When my heart is free from sorrow.

Like his beloved Byron, J. Gordon departed this vale of tears at thirty-six years of age. Fortunately for us Cooglerites, during those final six years, he collected and published many volumes of *Purely Original Verse*. Each volume was dedicated to his friends and benefactors: "my patrons throughout the North, East, and West"; "W. H. Gibbes Jr. and J. Wilson Gibbes"; "the Sons and Daughters of South Carolina"; "The J. Gordon Coogler Club, Stanza 1, of Atlanta, Georgia."

As the bard himself so aptly expresses in his introduction, "My style and my sentiments are MY OWN, purely original." Success and fame were immediate—not just in his native city, where the local newspaper regularly published his annual Christmas poem, but throughout the nation and even in England, as evidence here by the twenty-eight pages of excerpts from enthusiastic reviews. Coogler delighted in showing the clippings to all who entered his print shop, apparently accepting the tributes with complete sincerity. So moved was he by support from Editor Henry W. Grady that he dedicated his fifth edition to the Atlanta Coogler Club and sent the group an inscribed copy and a life-sized portrait.

Of course, there were a few fault-finding critics—like the one Coogler himself mentions: "a young lady who sought publicity by attempting to belittle in public print the author's poem 'Beautiful Snow' [the earlier quoted birdwatcher's couplet]. She has never been heard from through the press since." But the poet has made her immortal, though nameless:

> She died after the beautiful snow had melted,
>> And was buried beneath the "slush";
> The last sad words she breathed upon earth
>> Were these simple ones, "Oh, poet, do hush!"

Through all this recognition, Coogler remained a modest man, though frankly aware of his potential immortality:

You'll never see this head too large for my hat,
    You may watch it and feel it as oft as you choose;
But you'll learn as millions of people have learned,
    Of my character and name thro' my innocent muse.

You'll never see this form clad in gaudy apparel,
    Nor these feet playing the "dude" in patent-leather shoes;
But your children's children will some day read
    Some pleasant quotations from my innocent muse.

In financial gain he was also a success. His earliest volumes were paper pamphlets, selling for 50 cents each. From 1897 to his death in 1901 volumes of his complete works were bound and sold for $1 each ($1.10 by mail). According to his own records and the Columbia *State* obituary notice, over 5,000 copies of Coogler's *Purely Original Verse* were sold, and over 4,000 of these went outside the South. Income from his book sales (not including fees for "Poems Written While You Wait") was about $3,600—especially impressive at a time when corn was 30 cents a bushel and potato bugs had become a burden.

One of Coogler's contemporaries has characterized the bard as "that funny little serious fellow who wrote verses and rode a bicycle." An incurable romantic, he wrote many love poems, the first when he was a school boy, "To Minnie," who—as he later noted—went to Galveston and was drowned in a hurricane. Though he called on many lassies and wrote versified tributes, he never married. Few took seriously the gaunt figure with the monotonous voice.

But he himself took seriously his obligations to his church (he taught Sunday school at Washington Street Methodist Church) and his family (he was the sole support of his mother and three sisters). Income from his tiny little print shop and from his successful poetic ventures made life a little easier for him and his family.

His beloved mother died July 10, 1899, after a long illness. A month later, on August 17, his favorite and youngest sister Leonora died unexpectedly from a seemingly minor illness. Coogler himself was in poor health. He became haggard, emaciated, yet continued to try to do his work at the print-shop. Finally he took to his bed, and four days later he died. It was perhaps prophetic that the final poem he published was "Let Me Hang Up My Harp."

The Bard of the Congaree was buried at Columbia's Elmwood Cemetery, with Rev. M. L. Carlisle of Washington Street Methodist Church conducting the impressive service before a large crowd. The simple gravestone is marked:

J. GORDON COOGLER
Son of Samuel and Luana Coogler
Born Dec. 3, 1865
Died Sept. 9, 1901
He Uttered Nothing Base
Coogler

That Coogler's *Purely Original Verse* has been so long out of print is regrettable. There is some consolation for us Coogler fans that his name was early introduced into the language. Long before the now household words like *quisling, lollobrigidian,* and *Watergate,* there was *cooglerism*—used far and wide to mean "a solemn absurdity." Though Mencken's quote of the Coogler couplet ("Alas, for the South! . . .") obviously did not have immortality as his intent, the result has been just that.

Answering popular demand in the midst of the Coogler revival, we remember Dana's observation: "The country owes much to J. Gordon Coogler." Perhaps this reprint will repay some of that debt.

—Claude Henry Neuffer & Rene LaBorde

University of South Carolina
Columbia, S. C.

PURELY ORIGINAL VERSE.

COMPLETE WORKS,

AND A NUMBER OF NEW PRODUCTIONS,

IN ONE VOLUME.

BY

J. GORDON COOGLER,

COLUMBIA, S. C.

REVISED, ILLUSTRATED AND PUBLISHED BY THE AUTHOR.

———

Price $1.00.   By Mail, post-paid, $1.10.

1897.

THE AUTHOR'S EARLY HOME NEAR COLUMBIA.

Farewell, sweet home of my childhood hours!
  Where joy and sorrow were blended;
Within thy halls I have loved and lost,
  But now those scenes are ended.

[Page 43.]

CONTENTS.

CONTENTS

CONTENTS.

CONTENTS

INTRODUCTION.

Having been very successful in the past with my poetical works, it gives me pleasure to place in the hands of an appreciative public this volume containing my entire works, (consisting of five volumes) revised, with many of my latest unpublished productions.

I have been very much gratified at the appreciation shown my works in the past. The many lengthy and complimentary magazine and newspaper editorial reviews accorded my works throughout this entire country, have stimulated me to no little extent, and assured me of the success of this volume. I desire to tender to them my thanks and appreciation for their kind treatment of same.

I have given each poem in this volume my profound attention. Have consumed much midnight oil in trying to do justice to the subjects which lay nearest to my heart and inspired me to write.

I have disposed of more than 2,800 copies of my five small volumes. They have been in demand not only in the South, but throughout the North.

In presenting this volume I shall repeat the words contained in the introduction of my former ones: "My style and my sentiments are MY OWN, purely original."

I shall not attempt to quote all of the many lengthy reviews given my past works by the press at large—or the numerous complimentary letters received from literary persons throughout the country—as they would more than fill this volume. I shall give only a few extracts from some of the leading periodicals, beginning with "MUNSEY'S MAGAZINE," October, 1896. Their review I shall give in full as follows :

"J. GORDON COOGLER, POET LAUREATE.

"It is with no little confidence that we submit to an appreciating public the name of J. Gordon Coogler, the Sweet Singer of South Carolina, as a candidate for the position of American poet laureate. That the United States have never yet been able to boast an officially recognized national bard has seemed to us a matter for regret. The time seems ripe for the conferring of such an honor, and we know of no one upon whom it can more justly be bestowed than upon Mr. Coogler. As yet but little is known of this poet who is wasting his sweetness upon the desert air, but it will be unnecessary to do more than direct attention to his work to secure for him the reputation which he deserves.

His latest volume of poems is four inches wide by five and three quarter inches long and one quarter inch thick; it is bound in blue paper, and printed by the author; and we are informed by the introduction that it is the fourth of a series, completing more than four hundred compositions. We shall never cease to reproach ourselves for not having become familiar with Mr. Coogler's work before. His poems are of the lyrical order and display a marked ability in the matter of rhyme, tempered with a pleasing pessimism. As he says in his preface, 'My style and my sentiments are my own, purely original. I have borrowed no words intentionally from any author.' One has only to read these verses to be convinced that this claim is absolutely accurate. The laureate thus addresses his critics:

"Challenge me to fight on the open field,
 And hurl at my head the fiery dart,
Rather than belittle the gentle muse
 That ushers from this lonely heart.

"It must indeed be a captious reviewer who cannot frankly admire the charming simplicity and pastoral beauty of Mr. Coogler's poetry. Witness what may be done in the way of rhyming if one has only the divine afflatus, and witness also the peculiar pathos of the thought:

"From early youth to the frost of age
Man's days have been a mixture
Of all that constitutes in life
A dark and gloomy picture.

"Good as this is, however, it is not in philosophical quatrains that the poet reaches his highest level, but rather in lyrics that deal with the tender passion. In the poem entitled 'To Miss Mattie Sue' we have a use of the verb 'do' which commands immediate attention:

"As the summer sunbeams
Peep o'er the distant hills
On some sweet and lonely brook,
So my weary, longing eyes,
Warm with the dew of love,
To thee alone do look.

"On thy rosebud cheeks
Girlhood's sweetest smiles
In brightest hope do beam.

"And here is a combination of grammar, morality, and melody equally noticeable:

"On thy fair finger, lovely maiden,
Let there no jewel ever be
If character be put at stake
For the diamond ring he gives thee.

"Further extracts are perhaps unnecessary. We consider that those we have made are abundantly sufficient to support J. Gordon Coogler's candidacy for the title of American laureate. There have been native poets deserving of recognition. Longfellow, Whittier, Bryant, Holmes, Lovell—all these did fair work, 'but they have passed from our midst.' Where are we to look for one who shall celebrate American love, morals, and patriotism? There is but one answer to the question. J. Gordon Coogler, of Columbia, South Carolina, is alone worthy of being crowned with wreaths of bay. What his future is to be is best expressed in his own words (never borrowed 'intentionally from any author'):

"On every hill top, far and near,
He'll sing that sinful hearts might hear
His sweet refrain;
All men will bow before his face,
Whose winning smiles and perfect grace,
Will dispel all pain!"

Extracts from a page of editorial review of my third
volume, contained in "Puck," Nov. 7, 1894, entitled,

"THE GENIUS OF COOGLER.

"We have received a little volume entitled 'Poems by J. Gordon Coogler, Columbia, South Carolina,' with a request from the author to 'please
notice.' Book reviews are not in our line, but a careful study of these
poems has convinced us that their gifted author is really in need of some
fearless criticism, and he shall have it. Although we may be frank to the
verge of severity, it must be understood that we have no wish to belittle
the undoubted genius of Mr. Coogler. Rather would we indicate seem-
lier angles and free it from what we feel sure is a taint of insincerity.

*   *   *   *

"We repeat, that we do not wish to be needlessly harsh with Mr. Coogler, naught but a stern sense of justice and the conviction that we may be
of use to him prompts us to score him. . . . . Here, for instance, is the
influence of the improper Mr. Swinburne:

> "I could n't but love her snowy neck,
> In beauty grand without a speck
> Or trace at all;
> And looking then at her pretty feet,
> I praised that lower gift complete
> And very small.

> "Like the leaves of the summer rose
> Were her pink cheeks and pretty nose,
> Just simply grand.

"And again:

> "Many a Sabbath hour I've spent
> With Maud beside my knee,
> Gazing o'er the distant hills
> On the banks of the Congaree.

> "Many a balmy kiss I've stolen
> From precious lips too pure for me,
> While caressing lovely little Maud
> On the banks of the Congaree.

"We will not say that the tone of these verses is immoral, but surely
it is not elevating and ennobling. It is too suggestive.

"Here are some detached bits that show unmistakably the baneful
domination of Robert Browning:

> "I feel like some lone deserted lad
> Standing on the shore of life's great ocean,
> Casting pebbles in its billows,
> As if to excite some past emotion.

> "There's nothing in life to live for,
> Except it be sorrow and pain;
> But there's more in death than dying
> To simply exist again.

"It is in his poems dealing with death that Mr. Coogler strikes his truest note. Here is a fragment from 'Two Loved Ones in Heaven; written on the death of two lovely girls who passed away a short time since in this city.':

> "Their days were too few to be ended so soon
> By death's cold hand ere the fullness of noon;
> And e'en tho' fever was burning their cheek
> Of their heavenly home they did frequently speak.

> *   *   *   *

"Wretched taste we think is shown in some 'Lines to Byron.':

> "Oh, thou immortal Byron,
> Thy grand, inspired genius
> Let no man dare to smother;
> May all that was good within thee
> Be attributed to heaven;
> All that was evil—to thy mother.

"Byron's mother may not have been an admirable woman; she may have had the gravest of faults, but she died many years ago, and we protest that J. Gordon Coogler has no right to rake up any old scandal about her, especially in an ode to her talented son. Let the dead past, we say, bury its dead. Let us not, Mr. Coogler, be cruel and vindictive toward one who, whatever her failings, was once a woman. Remember your own 'Lines to Woman,' on p. 57:

> "Oh, that inexhaustible subject
> Filled with celestial fire
> On which no seraph's song can cease,
> No poet's pen expire.

"Many of his verses hint at a past eventful with grave transgressions:

> "There was a time when the fire of youth
> Burned deep within my wayward soul;
> I often stroll'd o'er pleasant hills
> Where timid mortals seldom stroll.

"Here and there is indicated an almost offensive vein of frivolity; but this is more than atoned for by a spirit of manliness which is admirably shown in the following:

"A MISTAKE.

"The poem containing three verses, published in my second book, and entitled 'That Christmas Card,' are the only verses in my life which I regret ever having written. The entire poem is a mistake, caused by being too hasty.

> "I would willingly forfeit my right to the Muse
> If I only this day could recall
> The verses I wrote in the heat of my passion,
> Which I consider the meanest of all.

"A manly and courageous amende, Mr. Coogler; you are the better for having made it.

"As a frontispiece to his little volume, Mr. Coogler prints a tasteful, half-tone engraving of himself. He is a fine, manly-looking young fellow of some twenty-nine or thirty, with a broad, high forehead, earnest deep-set eyes, prominent ears, and a small dark mustache. He is dressed in a neat, well-fitting suit of some dark shade. Of the quality of Mr. Coogler's verse, we prefer not to speak. As he says his style and his sentiments are his own; and who are we that we should say them well or ill?"

Extracts from nearly a page of editorial review of my fourth volume in the "LITERARY DIGEST," (N. Y.,) Nov. 2, 1895 :

"SOME PURELY ORIGINAL VERSE.

"Such are the 'poems' of J. Gordon Coogler, of Columbia, S. C., whose new book, being his fourth volume, has just reached us. In his 'Introduction,' Mr. Coogler says: 'In issuing this volume I shall repeat the words contained in the introduction in my last volume: My style and my sentiments are MY OWN, purely original.' We doubt if any one will question the truth of Mr. Coogler's strongly emphasized assertion. We admit that in the few choice extracts which we here present there is something which calls to mind, in a way, certain of the masters, but there is no sign of imitation. One cannot help thinking how Dr. Holmes or Mr. Lowell would have revelled in these rich stanzas, without ever accusing the author of plagiarizing their own or any other poet's lines.

"Mr. Coogler will doubtless have his adverse critics, as all poets have. Indeed, he has anticipated such in the following lines:

> "TO THE YOUNG UNJUST CRITIC.

> "Challenge me to fight on the open field,
> And hurl at my head the fiery dart,
> Rather than belittle the gentle muse
> That ~~ushers~~ from this lonely heart.

"Mr. Coogler cannot properly be called an optimist, for he has written the saddest kind of verse, yet he occasionally trills a merry lay, such as 'On the Cars to Shandon.' And by the way he has in this dainty madrigal entered quite a new field of song. It has been prophesied that the poetry of the future would treat on scientific themes; here we have it.

*   *   *   *

"The poet's deep earnestness of purpose is expressed in this quatrain:

> " 'Tis better this hand was silent,
> This mind obscure and weak,
> Than it should pen a single line
> These lips would dare not speak.

"And the following shows to what lofty height of diction his muse is capable of soaring:

> "Oh, character! thou ever art
> An holy and an honor'd thing;
> More valuable than life itself,
> ·More costly than a diamond ring."

"THE BOOKMAN," of New York, in nearly a column of review of my fifth volume, says:

"We were going to write quite a lengthy review of this inimitable little volume; but the author has made such a thing practically impossible by reprinting in the Introduction a collection of the comment and commendations already bestowed upon his verse by the most eminent critics from Dill Nye to the literary editor of MUNSEY's. These comments so perfectly anticipate all we should ourselves have said as to make it needless for us to do more than subscribe to them as expressing our sentiments exactly. . . . .

"We trust that this fifth volume of his verse may have many successors; and we are pretty sure it will, for a little poem we cull from page 28, is fraught with golden promise for the future:

> "You may as well try to change the course
> Of yonder sun
>   To north and south,
> As to try to subdue by criticism
> This heart of verse,
>   Or close this mouth."

12

Extracts from three pages of editorial review in "THE
NICKEL MAGAZINE," Boston, Mass., May, 1897, entitled,

"A GENIUS IN BLOOM.

"It is much the fashion nowadays to be loftily impatient with American poets. Indeed one hears from those who should know better that
America has no poet worthy of the name. But how insipidly conven-
tional, how ignobly superficial is the dictum! For America has poets
in abundance who sing potently in all the voices; but too often they
charm only a small circle, and are tricked by circumstance out of that
larger audience to which their genius and acquirements entitle them.
Steadfast in their ideals and constant in effort, they reck little of wide
fame or material rewards; they sing their lyrics and declaim their
epics, and the world may stop to listen if it will. If it will not—and too
often it does not—then the world, not the poet, is the loser. As a fine
type of these humbler bards, humble in pretension, not in achievement,
we present the name of J. Gordon Coogler, of Columbia, S. C. His fifth
and latest volume of poems has just come to us, and after reading it, we
hasten to do our little toward dispelling the obscurity with which a per-
verse fate has hitherto shrouded this genius of the Southland. Mr.
Coogler, it appears, is both a poet and a practical printer. As a critic,
whom he quotes in the introduction to the present volume, remarks:
'None other can conduct his muse all the way from the frowning heights
of Olympus to the tender clasp of a half-medium job press.' Unique in
this twinship, the poet is his own publisher, and that modesty which is
one of his salient attributes, has prompted him to put out all five of his
volumes in unassuming paper binding. The latest is entitled 'Purely
Original Verse.' In truth, originality would appear to be a hobby with him
if so transcendent a genius may be supposed to possess a thing so common.
'My style and my sentiments are MY OWN, purely original,' he insists
further; and an examination of his work proves this to be no idle boast.
To sense the full sweep of his power, it may be well to glance at some of
his earlier work before considering his latest. One is much struck first
by the spirit of intrepid, nay, almost aggressive defiance, with which he
dares the horde of unappreciative critics:

> "Challenge me to fight on the open field,
> And hurl at my head the fiery dart,
> Rather than belittle the gentle muse
> That ushers from this lonely heart.

"Next we are permitted to discover a not unpleasing pessimism joined to a facility of rhyme that is truly impressive:

> "From early youth to the frost of age
>   Man's days have been a mixture
> Of all that constitutes in life
>   A dark and gloomy picture.

"In his adaptation of certain verbs Coogler is both masterly and original.

*   *   *   *

But it is not alone in grammar that Coogler blazes new paths. In that species of analysis which is part metaphysics and part sentiment, a line which Robert Browning essayed with fairly creditable results, Coogler is especially happy, as in the following quotation:

> "I feel like some lone, deserted lad
>   Standing on the shore of life's great ocean,
> Casting pebbles in its billows,
>   As if to excite some past emotion.

*   *   *   *

"Coogler's later volume contrasts pleasantly with his earlier works. It is riper and more mature. While he consistantly preserves those quaint gramatical involutions and twists, he sees with clearer eyes, and pictures with a firmer touch the great arcana of humanity. In 'The Path to Fame,' the first poem of this volume, he again sounds his note of defiance to the critics, yet it has a gentler resonance than his earlier challenge:

> "The clouds may be dark that linger around
>   These feet as they move in that lone sphere,
> And the thorns be many to pierce my heart,
>   Yet 'mid all these I've nothing to fear.

> "Let critics assail my innocent muse,
>   And belittle the name which they ne'er can mar,
> Yet both shall shine from the hills of fame
>   Like the radiant light of some sweet star.

"While a deep-hued pessimism may be thought to color this volume, it is still far from morbid. Thus, in 'They Laid Her Down in a Lonely Grave,' the sadness of the theme is mitigated by a perception of the laws of nature which is both rational and reassuring:

> "They laid her down while the autumn leaves were falling,
>   In a lonely grave beside the deep blue sea;
> Her angel spirit is now beyond recalling,
>   And her fair form can ne'er revisit you and me,

"Is it any wonder that South Carolina's poet is able to sell 2.000 copies of his "purely original" verse at 50 cents a copy and then write more?"

Extracts from over a column of editorial review of my works in "THE PROVIDENCE (R. I.) JOURNAL":

"Genius will out. Even the seclusion of Columbia, S. C., cannot hide it. Mr. J. Gordon Coogler has issued four volumes of poetry, and has had the honor of long reviews from Puck and other serious organs of criticism, and yet we have waited for his fifth volume to make his acquaintance. The loss is ours and we hasten to repair it, assuring our readers with the utmost earnestness of which we are capable that a new fount of the purest literary delight awaits them in the pages of the modest paper-covered book, which the author has sent us with the request, 'Please notice.' Who could fail to notice a new note in the poetry of the time so penetrating as Coogler's? If he sang on some lone isle in the Pacific he would make himself heard.

*   *   *   *   *

"There is naturally much about the fair sex in this little volume; the great poetic heart has ever a keen longing to love and to be loved. Lines to 'A Golden Haired Girl,' to one whose 'gentle name was Maud,' 'To Lilian,' lines 'written on hearing a lady, speaking of her past hopes. say, 'I am now on the verge of womanhood; only eighteen summers old; but, oh, how unsteady I stand'—things like these cannot be found in ordinary volumes of verse. One of the poems which has interested us most gives a charming picture of social life in the fair Southern city. From the beginning—

"Down beside a clump of roses,
   Just beyond the garden wall,
Sat a little brown-eyed maiden,
   Waiting for her beau to call.

"Through the passionate longing of the heroine for the hero's arrival—

"Oh. I hear his footsteps coming,
   See the light of his cigar,
How it shines within the darkness
   Like some softly glowing star.

*   *   *   *

"But Mr. Coogler does not confine himself to the fair ones who move high in social circles. 'Sweet working girl,' he cries:

"I love to view the happy smiles
Upon thy fair and beaming face.

"And then he adds this word of encouragement:

"Sweet working girl—tho' Fate has destined thy fair hand
To labor in place of a wayward brother,
Yet Heaven will reward thee for thy honest toil
In support of thy aged, widow'd mother.

        *   *   *   *

"We must stop somewhere, fascinating as Mr. Coogler's volume is.
And we shall stop without a word of comment. Why gild refined gold
or paint the lily?"

Extracts from editorials in "THE (N. Y.) SUN":

"Our esteemed contemporary, the 'Carolina Spartan' imparts the glad
news that J. Gordon Coogler, the poet laureate of Columbia, has published the fifth volume of his poems. J. Gordon Coogler, as his admirer
well remarks is 'bold enough to attempt flights heretofore unessayed,
and he writes verse as no other man has ever written.' The country
owes much to J. Gordon Coogler. . . . . No cotton is softer or gentler
than are his Arcadian songs. J. Gordon Coogler has often been called
the Sir Edward Arnold of Columbia."

Again "THE SUN" says:

"J. Gordon Coogler of Columbia, the great bard of the Palmetto State,
is described by our contemporary, the 'Galveston News.' 'as having a
fine mouth, a set to either jaw that indicates great physical firmness,
the eye of an eagle, the nose of a Roman.' This is not meant to be unjust, but it is not entirely exact. Mr. J. Gordon Coogler has the eye of
a falcon rather than that of the eagle, the nose of a pelasgian, the mouth
of a nightingale, the chin of a lark, and his jaw is melodious like a harp
in flesh. His sentiments are as sound and his conjugations are as original as his lineaments are imposing. Who except Coogler is capable of
singing:

"On thy fair finger. lovely maiden,
Let there no jewel ever be
If character be put at stake
For the diamond ring he gives thee."

And again "THE SUN" says:

"Mr. J. Gordon Coogler, the sweet singer of the South Carolina cotton

The "CHAP BOOK," of Chicago, Ill., in quite a lengthy review of my fifth volume, says :

"'Impossible,' is the title of Mr. J. Gordon Coogler's apt poem, big with undiluted truth.

*   *   *   *

"But it is after all to some of Mr. Coogler's five volumes that the illuminati have been, . . accustomed to turn for diversion. He takes for his theme, 'Maud, the Mill, and the Lily,' and the following stanza results ;

> "There flows the same familiar stream,
>   Whose waters I oft have drank ;
> And the old mill-pond. from whose dark edge
>   I oft, so oft have shrank.

"Or says, 'Farewell Sweet College Girl!' thus:

> "Farewell! ye milk-white dove, farewell!
>   If on earth we meet no more,
> May in that snow-white throng of love
>   We meet on yonder shore.

"But it is not alone in the young woman of grace and culture that the poet sees a suitable theme : witness his lines to 'The Working Girl :

> "Sweet working girl—tho' Fate has destined thy fair hand
>   To labor in place of a wayward brother,
> Yet Heaven will reward thee for thy honest toil
>   In support of thy aged, widowed mother."

Extracts from nearly a column of editorial review of my works in the "CLEVELAND (Ohio) WORLD":

"SOUTH CAROLINA'S POET.

"We beg leave to acknowledge a volume of poems by J. Gordon Coogler, the poet laureate of South Carolina. Mr. Coogler not only writes his own poems, but he sets them into type and sees that they are properly printed in his own printing office. His home is at Columbia, South Carolina, and this is the fifth volume of his poetic efforts he has given to the public. . . . . . .

"The econiums of praise that have been heaped upon Mr. Coogler by the press of the country have been most flattering, to him, and highly enjoyable to everybody else.

"Mr. Coogler's style is certainly simple, and not bound down by any iron clad rules of prosody or meter. The rapturous beauty of the sentiment which is 'purely original' oozes forth from the almost inspired words of this poet of South Carolina. What can be more delicate in its simplicity, deep in its moral, or charming in its whole conception than the following entitled "Woman's Folly.':

> "Alas! poor woman, with eyes of sparkling fire,
> Thy heart is often won by mankind's gay attire;
> So weak thou art. so very weak at best,
> Thou canst not look beyond a satin-lined vest.
>
> "I've seen thee ofttimes cast a winning glance
> And be carried away—as it were within a trance—
> By the gay apparel of some dishonest youth,
> Whose bosom heaved with not a single truth.
>
> "Alas! for thee—I would that thou couldst learn
> That love does not in such quicksilver burn;
> That he who lurks beside thy virtuous path,
> When thy good name is gone, will gaze on thee and laugh.
>
> "For what care he, whom thy fair hand would take,
> If in after years thy gentle heart should break;
> No tears of remorse would damp his wayward eyes—
> Such tears can only come ere the conscience dies.

"It is our regret that it is not possible to give many examples of Mr. Coogler's poetry, but space does not permit. Yet one more sample might well be included. It is made up of two stanzas of a poem entitled, 'The Path to Fame,' and indicates that Mr. Coogler is adamant to the shafts of criticism if any should perchance be aimed in his direction:

> "Let critics assail my innocent muse,
> And belittle the name which they ne'er can mar,
> Yet both shall shine from the hills of fame
> Like the radiant light of some sweet star.
>
> "Tho' the course I have taken be lonely and dark,
> Pitied, condemned, by one and by all;
> Yet the star of ambition is glowing for me,
> Tho' I stumble alas! I ne'er shall fall.

14

"To him has come in these riper years a tolerant appreciation of the virtues and failings of the Eternal Feminine:

"Some day, when the gloomy shades of life shall have borne
The golden sunbeams from 'round your gentle feet,
Then you will think of the love which you have spurn'd
On my hearts pure shrine so gentle and so sweet.

* * * *

"In 'Woman's Folly' he scathingly yet justly rebukes her for that she judges man too often by his raiment:

"Alas! poor woman, with eyes of sparkling fire,
Thy heart is often won by mankind's gay attire;
So weak thou art, so very weak at best,
Thou canst not look beyond a satin-lined vest.

"I've seen thee ofttimes cast a winning glance
And be carried away—as it were within a trance—
By the gay apparel of some dishonest youth,
Whose bosom heaved with not a single truth.

"How true it is that woman often neglects to use the X-ray of her God-given intuition to pierce the sheen of a specious waistcoat and survey the hollowness it hides; and may we not feel a generous sympathy for this poet who has, all too plainly, seen true worth passed by for a gaudy exterior? But though he is often judicial to the verge of harshness, he does not lack a certain winning chivalry:

"Go shatter the walls of some beautiful city
That is noted for grandeur and fame,
Rather than cast a suggestive remark
To destroy a woman's fair name.

"And again:

"She's a polished, noble lady,
Highly learned, industrious, too,
And her sunny hand is faithful
In what e'er it finds to do.

"And not infrequently he shows both chivalry and humility:

"Maud—for her gentle name was Maud—
Wore many smiles, and they were sad;
A thousand virtues she retained,
Many of which I never had.

"But it is where his pen punctures social and political bubbles that he soars to his loftiest heights. Instance the delicate scorn tinged with yearning pity of the following lines:

"Alas! Carolina! Carolina! fair land of my birth.
  Thy fame will be wafted from the mountain to the sea
As being the greatest educational centre on earth,
  At the cost of men's blood thro' thy 'one X' whiskey.

"Two very large elephants thou hast lately installed,
  Where thy sons and thy daughters are invited to come,
And learn to be mentally and physically strong,
  By the solemn proceeds of thy 'innocent' rum.

"We have tried thus briefly to give some adequate notion of the genius of J. Gordon Coogler. His own low-looking, money-grabbing generation may not accord him his due; but we are confident that posterity will not fail in this respect. . . . . .

"Verily, we may say of this master of his own peculiar style, in closing this all-too-inadequate review of his works:

"Oh! worthy, worthy Bard!
  Of loftiest melody the puissant bugler!
We've much to cheer us e'en tho' times be bad,
  While our literary pantheon contains a Coogler."

"GODEY'S MAGAZINE," (that 'Edinburgh' of the present time) delights in condemning the work of young authors, as 'belonging to the class which neither gods nor men are said to permit.' For variety's sake, not truth and justice, I am glad that it exists, and I can hear from it occasionally.

Here are a few extracts from nearly a column of review it accorded my works:

"Mr. Coogler has just about become a national figure in contemporary literature. . . . . .
"Mr. Coogler, like Horace and others, is sublimely assured of his own immortality.
                    *   *   *   *
"And yet in the midst of all this hopeless banality and ignorance he came near writing something very fine in this six-line stanza—an undecimal couplet it is really:

"Ah, Daisy, so lovely in thy gentleness,
  Who would not press thy snowy hand
    Until thy cheeks grew red;
Who would not live in the balmy breeze
  That gently wafts the silken curls
    On thy angelic head."

fields, must look to his laurels. Another and a rival poet has appeared in Mr. Lewis M. Elshemus, whose native wood notes wild, sounded in two volumes entitled respectively, 'Lady Vere,' and 'Mammon—A Spirit Song' (Eastman Lewis), have much of the artless and unfettered originality that have made the Southern singer famous. We miss, perhaps, the infinite variety and range of vision that distinguish the inimitable Coogler."

"THE ATLANTA CONSTITUTION" says :

"Editor Dana, of 'THE SUN' is an ardent Cooglerite."

"THE KANSAS CITY (MO.) TIMES" says :

"Some of Mr. Coogler's work has been highly praised by a number of critics, and in his last volume he amply proves his poetic temperament. A number of his verses show true poetic expression. The fault with many of his verses lies in a hasty composition. From the good verses, Mr. Coogler proves that he can write well, so there is little excuse for the bad ones." . . . .

"THE INDIANAPOLIS (Indiana) JOURNAL" says :

"From the Sunny South comes the fifth volume of Mr. J. Gordon Coogler's 'Purely Original Verse.' It must indeed be a captious reader who could not frankly admire the charming simplicity and pastoral beauty of Mr. Coogler's poetry.

From quite a lengthy review in "THE HARTFORD (Conn.) COURANT":

"The fifth volume of 'Purely Original Verse,' by J. Gordon Coogler of Columbia, S. C., is one of those books which lend themselves so readily to quotation that it is very difficult to refrain from transcribing whole pages. Munsey's Magazine and Puck were unable to resist lengthy editorial comment.

*　　　*　　　*　　　*　　　*

"But we cannot allow ourselves to be led from page to page gathering blossoms. Suffice it to say that the author has seen life, that he knows friendship to be

"No Spirit from the heavens,
Nor the regions of the dead;
But a kind of unknown demon
Manufactured in the head."

From "THE MILWAUKEE (Wis.) JOURNAL":

"Mr. Coogler's verses remind one of the choice specimens of Mr. Gifted Hopkins' muse which Dr. Holmes has given us in 'The Guardian Angel.' In his introduction to the little book, which is the fifth volume of Mr. Coogler's work, the poet gratefully acknowledges the many complimentary notices which his previous volumes have received. Extracts are given from reviews which have appeared in Puck and other journals. Bill Nye is numbered among the admirers of Mr. Coogler who have written facetiously and appreciatively of his muse. Among the most touching of the poems we may mention: 'Ah, Daisy'; 'Other Days;' 'Think of Me;' 'Willie is Gone;' 'She's Ill,' and 'The Mysterious Tear.' In spite of the allurements of fame, the poet maintains a becoming modesty of spirit, as the following lines show:

"If I should rise to lofty heights,
A humble heart shall be thereon;
And though you may be far below,
Remember, you I shall not scorn."

From over a column of review in "THE PITTSBURG (Pa.) TIMES":

"Here is a poetic outfit to begin with that has scarcely ever been surpassed, and it is not surprising, therefore, that the volume Mr. Coogler requests 'THE TIMES' to notice is the fifth that has come from his inspired pen.

* * * *

"The following stanza which is put in as a 'filler' at the bottom of one of the pages expresses the deep and permanent sadness of his great mind:

"In the deepest recesses of my heart there's a gloom
Which keeps me eternally sad;
Yet the smiles of my face and the words of my mouth
Are always cheerful and glad.

"That he has a great mind for the play of human emotions is certified in the following fragment:

"The mind that cannot create worlds,
　　Make hills and mountains great or small,
And streams and lakes, and thus the like,
　　Is to my mind—no MIND at all.
　　　　　*　　　　　*　　　　　*

"In spite of his constitutional sadness he sings much of love; but it is unrequitted love. Notwithstanding his love for women he is severe upon their follies, and thus expresses his condemnation:

"Alas! poor woman, with eyes of sparkling fire,
　Thy heart is often won by mankind's gay attire;
So weak thou art, so very weak at best,
　Thou canst not look beyond a satin-lined vest.

"But it would be futile within the limit of this review to attempt to point out all the beautiful notes of this dulcet-voiced singer of Dixie. We must leave something for the reader."

Extracts from a lengthy review in "THE NEWARK (N. J.) ADVERTISER":

"Love! To what heights of rapture, and abysses of despair does the tenderest yet cruelest of passion not raise or plunge this honey-lipped singer of the Congaree?:

"Oh, that inexhaustible subject
　Filled with celestial fire
On which no seraph song can cease,
　No poet's pen expire.
　　　　　*　　　　　*　　　　　*

"Mr. Coogler's opinions on subjects on which poets have written before, but never as he does are interesting. Here are some of the pearls of thought he scatters broadcast with prodigal hand:

"Oh, character! thou ever art
　An holy and an honor'd thing;
More valuable than life itself,
　More costly than a diamond ring.
　*　　　　　*　　　　　*　　　　　*

"All heaven has no water soft enough,
　Nor earth no cleansing soap,
That can wash the crimson from the heart
　That destroys a woman's hope.

"Observe how deftly the plainest every-day thing, such as soap, is woven into the web of verse. Mr. Coogler's range of subjects is as illimitable as the infinite. Versatility is his forte. Now, here, now there, he seems everywhere at once."

Extracts from a column of review in "THE LOUISVILLE (Ky.) COURIER JOURNAL":

"The poets of these degenerate days are, as a rule, a meek, downtrodden lot. whom one may ridicule with impunity. One notable exception, however, is J. Gordon Coogler, of Columbia, S. C., the distincton between him and the general run of singers being so marked as to lead to grave doubts as to his being a genuine poet. Would a genuine modern poet have had the temerity to address such a stanza as this to the critics?:

> "Challenge me to fight on the open field,
> And hurl at my head the fiery dart,
> Rather than belittle the gentle muse
> That trances from this lonely heart.

"Yet in this very boldness lies the secret of Mr. Coogler's success.

* * * *

"It is but fair to state that here and there lines of beauty are to be found in the work. . . . . . His position is unique. His work has been widely read, and has been given more attention by some of the leading newspapers and periodicals than that of men of real genius. In so far as being known as a writer is concerned, he is famous."

"THE MINNEAPOLIS (Minn.) JOURNAL" in a column of review says:

"'Purely Original Verse,' by a South Carolina poet. J. Gordon Coogler. It is really exhilarating to read such a title. What the reading public in this country has long been looking for is a new American poet who will give them 'purely original verse.' The information is also given that this is the fifth volume of Mr. Coogler's poetry. . . . He has disposed of over 2,000 copies, and adds: 'My style and my sentiments are my own, purely original.' And this South Carolina genius does not forget to give us a full-page portrait of himself, a young man with dark hair, carefully pointed mustache, sitting at a table, his eyes 'with fine frenzy rolling,' writing one of his 'purely original poems.' Not only this, but Mr. Coogler gives a picture of 'the author's early home near Columbia, S. C.,' the birth place of this extraordinary genius.

* * * *

> "Let critics assail my innocent muse,
> And belittle the name which they ne'er can mar,
> Yet both shall shine from the hills of fame
> Like the radiant light of some sweet star.

"This is bumptiuous, if not heroic; but Mr. Coogler is more positive about his fame when he says:

> "You may as well try to change the course
>   Of yonder sun
>   To north and south,
> As to try to subdue by criticism
>   This heart of verse,
>   Or close this mouth.

"Well, it looks like it, since Mr. Coogler has issued five volumes of his verse. There will be little use to try to shut him up. Mr. Coogler has evidently been heels over head in love with the South Carolina maidens, for he addresses numerous allusions to them. For instance, in a poem to 'Lilian,' he says:

> "Yet the love which you have taught me
>   Ne'er shall fade within my breast,
> But shall beam along my journey
>   Like a sunbeam from the west.

*   *   *   *

"Mr. Coogler cannot like Keats, be tortued or slain by adverse comment."

From a lengthy editorial in "THE ATLANTA (Ga.) CONSTITUTION":

"Our readers have no doubt heard of J. Gordon Coogler, the able young poet, whose pleasing fancies have won for him a fame that is unique in this age of cold commercial transactions. There must be something in the writings of a man who can attract attention and win applause when corn is thirty cents a bushel and potato bugs have become a burden.

*   *   *   *   *

":It will be the chief distinction of those who gird at J. Gordon Coogler that they are unable to see what posterity will see so plainly. Meanwhile, the work of Cooglerising the country is rapidly growing and spreading. Enthusiastic Cooglerites are springing up everywhere, and Cooglerisms are heard on every side. These things show the drift of popular sentiment and taste."

Again "THE CONSTITUTION" says, in a column of review of my works:

"By his works ye shall know an author, and it would require a calm perusal of the five volumes issued by J. Gordon Coogler in order to get in touch with the delicate fibers of his thoughts and feel the real force of his undoubted genius. It was Carlyle who said of Burns: 'He had a soul like an Aeolian harp changing the vulgar wind into melody.' Would that Carlyle could have known J. Gordon Coogler.

"In 'Maud, the Mill. and the Lily' a few of the most passionate thoughts of Mr. Coogler find utterance. It has about it the soleful symphony of Tennyson's 'Maud' as shown by the following verse:

> "Maud—for her gentle name was Maud—
>   Wore many smiles, and they were sad.
> A thousand virtues she retained,
>   Many of which I never had.

"After a full description of Maud he gives the following graphic picture:

> "Maud did not heed the roaring sound
>   Of distant thunder in the west,
> Nor did she fear the lightning's flash
>   Glistening on her snowy breast.

"In individualizing Mr. Coogler gives highest respect to woman, but for woman in the abstract he sometimes shows peculiar antipathy.

*   *   *   *

"On this same subject of woman Mr. Coogler has a poem called 'She Fell Like a Flake of Snow.' In this stanza the pathos is most keen:

> "She was beautiful once; but she fell.
>   And some said: 'Let her go,
> For she can never shine again
>   Like a beautiful flake of snow.'

"These few selections give but a faint idea of the genius of the South Carolina laureate."

———

"THE COLUMBIA (S. C.) STATE" in a lengthy editorial review says:

"Coogler's fifth volume of 'Purely Original Verse' is already recognized by eutomological criticism throughout this broad land as a new and distinct species of surpassing interest.

"There is but one Coogler, the founder of the Cooglerian school of poesy, and while he sings the great American people will listen to no other of his kind. Later, perhaps, when Coogler shall have hung up his lyre, and reclined upon his couch of bays, his pupils will begin to pipe—but not now, not yet. He has founded his school, established his cult."

"THE CHICAGO (Ill.) POST" in a column of editorial review, says:

"J. Gordon Coogler of South Carolina, the sweet singer of the Saluda, who reasonably aspires to the mantle worn by Paul Hayne, Lanier and Father Ryan, has favored us with a copy of his 'purely original verse.'

             *   *   *   *

· · · "We have pursued his flights of fancy with more than ordinary interest, and with an effort to be calmly logical, though just and appreciative. We opened the book at 'Woman's Folly,' and as we are always concerned over the follies of woman we attach great importance to Mr. Coogler's conclusions.

        *   *   *   *   *

"Our next experience with Mr. Coogler's verse was the passionate adieu, 'Farewell Lilian':

> "Farewell. Lilian, you are going
> Far away to leave me now;
> You shall be the sunlight, Lilian,
> That shall linger on my brow.

    *   *   *   *   *

"But Mr. Coogler is not solely devoted to his 'Lilian,' for we find him invoking 'Maud,' 'Daisy' and 'Laura,' not to speak of 'a golden-haired girl,' a 'brown-eyed lady who occupies a lovely cottage,' a 'sweet college girl,' otherwise known as a 'milk-white dove,' and an inamorata who 'is lying ill at her home.' And Mr. Coogler is not bound down by any hampering laws of caste, for he has an eye and a heart for the 'poor working girls,' as this lyric betrays:

> "Sweet working girl, I love to view the happy smiles
> Upon thy fair and beaming face;
> Thy perfect form, tho' devoid of rich apparel,
> Is lovelier far because of its simple grace.

"There's gallantry for you! Petrarch never wrote a prettier thing to his Laura, nor Swift to his Stella, nor Dante to his Beatrice, nor Artie to his Min. But we must pass swiftly and regretfully away from these tender outpourings to the contemplation of Mr. Coogler's philosophy as portrayed in 'Marriage and Death':

> "Marriage and death—these great events in life,
> Alas! with each other are blended;
> A festive scene and a funeral march,
> And man's brief journey is ended.

"A marriage puff and a funeral notice
Is the end of his transient tale,
And he vanishes from human sight
Beyond life's dark and gloomy veil.

"We had not intended at this time to speak so exhaustively of Mr. Coogler's achievements, but we have been carried away by sincere approbation of his poetic impulse. It remains for us to say only that Mr. Coogler's book is adorned with a very attractive picture of the poet himself, sitting at his table, pen in hand, thinking some thoughts of Maud and Daisy and Lilian, or, perchance throwing a fiery challenge at his envious contemporaries."

Editor Hale of "THE NASHVILLE (Tenn.) AMERICAN" concludes a column of review of my works as follows: (Speaking of the poem entitled "The Path to Fame," he says,)

"The courage displayed is sublime. Here is at least one more poet who would be willing, I opine, to die for Greece. But the public is so queer in its tastes!

"Seriously, if Mr. Coogler will study, acquaint himself with his technique, and then write something, he may, on the notice he is now receiving, be enabled to win a kinder public's ear than most young versifiers have won it. I at least wish him the fulfillment of his aspirations, as expressed in his lines to Hope:

"For me thou hast upon thy gilded beam,
The sunlight of a happier dream
Ere my days shall cease."

"THE RUTLAND (Vt.) HERALD" in over a column of strong editorial, entitled, "Two Kinds of Diplomacy," in which it deals with what the English papers say about the "'annoying ignorance of diplomatic methods' 'shown by Secretary of State Sherman in the Behring sea correspondence with Lord Salisbury," referring to myself, says:

"We are inclined to say with that able but not as yet very famous manufacturer of verse, J. Gordon Coogler, that

"The man who thinks God is too kind
To punish actions vile,
Is bad at heart, of unsound mind,
Or very juvenile."

From a column of editorial in the "ALBANY (N. Y.) ARGOSY":

"Mr. J. Gordon Coogler's fifth volume of 'Purely Original Verse' is a dainty volume of 82 pages, and contains more variety to the square inch than any other book of poems with which we have acquaintance. Verses of Mr. Coogler are certainly versatile.

    *   *   *   *   *

"Mr. Coogler is conscious of his failings, and in his poem of 'Maud, the Mill and the Lily,' he pays this tribute to Maud at his own expense:

> Maud—for her gentle name was Maud—
> Wore many smiles, and they were sad;
> A thousand virtues she retained,
> Many of which I never had.

    *   *   *   *   *

"We might continue indefinitely, but we close with the stanza entitled 'Impossible.' . . . .

"THE KNOXVILLE (Tenn.) TRIBUNE" in nearly a column of editorial says :

"Coogler is no weakling; not a poet to be bluffed by criticism, or driven into silence by contumelious remarks. He is as defiant as he is original. He is game; we admire his spirit, as we admire his verse."

"THE CHARLESTON (S. C.) NEWS AND COURIER" in a review of my works, says :

"There are many gems of thought and of melody scattered thoughout the pages of Mr. Coogler's volume. but we shrink from the task of selecting the few that our limit would permit, while leaving unmentioned so many others equally worthy of fame. We cannot, however, resist the temptation of giving our readers the benefit of one stanza, which seems to us to combine patriotism, poetry and satire in a quite remarkable degree. It is the first verse of the author's innovation to his native State:

> "Alas! Carolina! Carolina! Fair land of my birth.
> Thy fame will be wafted from the mountain to the sea,
> As being the greatest educational centre on earth.
> At the cost of men's blood thro' thy 'one X' whiskey."

From a page of review in "THE COLUMBIA (S. C.) REGISTER":

"All truly great minds have a way of striking the keynote of a subject in a single utterance, and without circumlocution of any kind; and the present reviewer was not, therefore, in the least surprised to find the very first poem in Mr. Coogler's fifth volume indicative of the pure and hallowed ambition that incites him to woo the muse. Its title is, 'The Path to Fame,' and the initial verse lets every intelligent reader into Mr. Coogler's secret:

> "The path is old and well-beaten I know
> That leads away o'er the hills to fame;
> I've started therein and I cannot turn back,
> I've naught to regret, and no one to blame."

"THE TRENTON (N. J.) TIMES" concluding an editorial on my works, says:

"It is difficult to assign J. Gordon Coogler to a place among the greater poets. His style seems to be a mixture of the Byronic and Tennysonian, though we do not wish to even intimate that Coogler is not original in his treatment of subjects."

Editor Chas. Petty of "THE CAROLINA SPARTAN" concludes an editorial, as follows:

"J. Gordon Coogler, with the greatest facility, born of inspiration, fills up the little space at the bottom of the pages of his volumes with dainty couplets like this:

> "Alas! for the South, her books have grown fewer—
> She never was much given to literature.

"Bravely does he stand up and plead that woman's fair fame shall never be stained by word or insinuation. He says:

> "All heaven has no water soft enough,
> Nor earth no cleansing soap,
> That can wash the crimson from the heart
> That destroys a woman's hope.

"Now if that is not poetry, we would like for some one to tell us what it is."

A literary critic in the "ALKAHEST," Atlanta, Ga., writes:

"I will confess I had been reading Coogler for several months in secret before I discovered that he was to be appreciated, to be applauded, to be perpetuated. The first thought of all this burned in upon me while I was reading for the eleventh time the poem entitled: 'I Dislike a Vain and Haughty Man.' It was after reading the fourth verse which is as follows, that I became purely enthused:

"If I should rise to lofty heights,
And humble heart shall be thereon,
And though you may be far below,
Remember, YOU I shall not scorn."

"THE SPARTANBURG (S. C.) HERALD" closes a lengthy editorial as follows:

"A prophet is not without honor save in his own country, and it is much the same with poets. While South Carolina and Boston are pouring over the satin-lined volumes of Browning, the great heart of the great West has responded to the modest little 'fifth volume of purely original verses,' and we begin to see grey streaks of the dawn of a Cooglerian age.'"

Quite a number of other journals and magazines have noticed my works, some of them very extensively; but space will not permit further extracts. Among them are:

"The Boston Journal," the "Colorado Springs Gazette," the "Denver Colorado Times," the "Evening Telegram," Portland, Oregon, the "Detroit Free Press," the "Omaha Bee," the Jacksonville (Fla.) Citizen," the "Norfolk (Va.) Landmark," the "Atlanta Journal," the "Savannah Morning News," the "Greenville (S. C.) News," and the "Ohio State Journal."

Among the magazines: "Peterson's Magazine," N. Y., "The Outlook," N. Y., "Book News," Philadelphia."

LETTERS FROM LITERARY PERSONS.

"1823 ALDINE AVENUE, CHICAGO, ILL., MARCH 25th, 1897.

Mr. J. Gordon Coogler, Columbia, S. C.:

DEAR SIR: I have been asked to write to you to express the deep interest taken in your work by one of Chicago's most celebrated literary clubs. We spent one whole evening of extreme enjoyment in reading and commenting upon your fifth volume of 'Purely Original Verse' and are now most anxious to know something more of one who has so aptly been called the American laureate. Other evenings of this season we have given over to the discussion of Heinrich Heine, Frederick Amiel and other writers of poetry and philosophy, but none has been so intensely enjoyable as that spent in the reading of your fifth volume of verse. We hope to spend next Thursday evening, April 1st, in another 'Coogler' evening and would like to have you send some of the earlier of your published works, as well as an extra two or three copies of volume five. Any information you care to add about how you came to discover your gift and what laurels, other than those you refer to in your introduction, have come to you from the public, we should be very, very grateful for. We regard you, if I may say so, as an extraordinary interesting man and would eagerly welcome any smallest detail of autobiographical information which might help us to a solution of the problem of your remarkable mentality.

Please forward the volumes, with bill for same, and any other contribution you may care to make toward our study of your muse, to Miss Elizabeth Abbott, 1823 Aldine Avenue, Chicago, Ill.

Yours very sincerely, with profound gratitude,

ELIZABETH ABBOTT."

The following letter was received from Mr. Henry W. Grady, Atlanta, Ga., president of the first literary club organized in my name in the South, on receiving a life-size portrait of myself and a copy of my complete works:

"ATLANTA, GA., JUNE 14th, 1897.

Mr. J. Gordon Coogler, Columbia, S. C.:

MY DEAR SIR: The morning's express brought to the Coogler club the elegant present you have so generously made the organization. To say that the members of the club are delighted with the picture and grateful for your interest in the organization but mildly expresses their feelings. Each and every member wanted to take the picture from the packing case with his own hands, but I, as president of the club, appointed myself a committee of one to perform that pleasant duty. The elegant little volume containing these poetic gems that we all love so dearly will be kept in the club room at all times where the members may learn something each day of their favorite poet. I trust that you will pardon a few words about myself, but I want you to know what a pleasure your poems have been to me personally. I read them constantly and at every perusal of your sweet verse I find something new to admire and sentiments that appeal to me. May your muse long continue to guide your fearless pen and give to the world, in spite of your envious critics, more of those charming verses that are making you immortal. But in my enthusiasm I have digressed from my intention of thanking you for the picture and the poems. I desire not only to thank you in behalf of the club, but to personally let you know how I, as president of the Coogler club, appreciate your interest in our little band. If the club can do anything, however small, in the way of making the world appreciate real genius, I can confidently say that every member will feel that he has done something to help the condition of his fellow man. The world will soon learn that the South has at least one literary genius who, though he may pass out of his mortal form, will ever live in the memory of his people as one worthy to represent to the world of letters a people proud to point to him as their one great poet. We have every day requests from people to become members of the club, but we are careful about admitting new brothers, as we have now an organization to be proud of and desire to have in it only the most appreciative literary spirits. As you know, nearly all of the members of the club are newspaper men who are working, as you are, to become famous with the pen, and who are ever ready to do what they can to aid their more fortunate brothers on up the road of fame.

With the best wishes of the club and its humble president, I have the honor to be your admirer and friend,

HENRY W. GRADY."

The following is an extract from a letter received by the author from a highly intelligent literary lady of Boston, Mass. Owing to the letter being of a private nature, her name is omitted :

"Through your kindness I can now enjoy the whole of the beautiful lyric beginning,

> "As the summer sunbeams
> Peep o'er the distant hills
>   On some sweet and lonely brook,
> So my weary, longing eyes,
> Warm with the dew of love,
>   To thee alone do look.

"But why so short ? You always stop when one wants you to go on the most. 'I Wish I Was There' is as beautiful as it is sad. Even the dear little 'Violet and Jonquil' has the tone-color of sadness."

(FIFTH VOLUME.)

———

This volume, (the fifth in order of a series of small volumes) containing seventy pages, I respectfully dedicate to

THE J. GORDON COOGLER CLUB, STANZA 1, OF ATLANTA, GA.,

as a token of gratitude for their appreciation of my works.

J. GORDON COOGLER.

COLUMBIA, S. C.

—————— • • • • ●●●●●● • • • ——————

(The dedication of each of the other small volumes in this volume complete will be as follows: Fourth volume; to the Sons and Daughters of Carolina—third volume; to my patrons throughout the North, East and West—second volume; to Dr. W. J. Murray—first volume; to W. H. Gibbes, Jr., and J. Wilson Gibbes.)

THE PATH TO FAME.

The path is old and well-beaten I know
  That leads away o'er the hills to fame;
I've started therein and I cannot turn back,
  I've naught to regret, and no one to blame.

The clouds may be dark that linger around
  These feet as they move in that lone sphere,
And the thorns be many to pierce my heart,
  Yet 'mid all these I've nothing to fear.

Let critics assail my innocent muse,
  And belittle the name which they ne'er can mar,
Yet both shall shine from the hills of fame
  Like the radiant light of some sweet star.

Tho' the course I have taken be lonely and dark,
  Pitied, condemn'd by one and by all;
Yet the star of ambition is glowing for me,
  Tho' I stumble, alas! I ne'er shall fall.

IMPOSSIBLE.

You may as well try to change the course
       Of yonder sun
           To north and south,
As to try to subdue by criticism
       This heart of verse,
           Or close this mouth.

WOMAN'S FOLLY.

Alas! poor woman, with eyes of sparkling fire,
Thy heart is often won by mankind's gay attire;
So weak thou art, so very weak at best,
Thou canst not look beyond a satin-lined vest.

I've seen thee ofttimes cast a winning glance
And be carried away—as it were within a trance—
By the gay apparel of some dishonest youth,
Whose bosom heaved with not a single truth.

Alas! for thee—I would that thou couldst learn
That love does not in such quicksilver burn;
That he who lurks beside thy virtuous path,
When thy good name is gone, will gaze on thee and laugh.

For what care he, whom thy fair hand would take,
If in after years thy gentle heart should break;
No tears of remorse would damp his wayward eyes—
Such tears can only come ere the conscience dies.

———

AH, DAISY.

Ah, Daisy, so lovely in thy gentleness,
Who would not press thy snowy hand
Until thy cheeks grew red;
Who would not live in the balmy breeze
That gently wafts the silken curls
On thy angelic head.

———

Alas! for the South, her books have grown fewer
She never was much given to literature.

SOME DAY.

Some day, when the light of your sweet azure eyes
　　Shall grow dim as dying sunbeams on the sea,
Then as you raise those weary eyes and gaze
　　Afar off—may you sometimes think of me.

Some day, when memory brings the happy thought
　　Of other years when our hearts beat firm and slow,
Then you may bear for me that perfect love
　　I have borne for you, since I met you long ago.

Some day, when life's dark shadows shall have borne
　　The golden sunbeams from 'round your gentle feet,
Then you will think of the love which you have spurn'd
　　On my heart's pure shrine, so gentle and so sweet.

May you, when the dint of sorrow marks your brow,
　　And hope grows dim within your troubl'd heart,
Think of me, alone in this changing world,
　　Mourning o'er love's ties, that now lie far apart.

Think, then, of the happy hours we've spent together
　　On the summit of yonder gentle hill,
Where in tears you told me you'd be true to me,
　　Those words burn deep within my mem'ry still.

Some day—if not within this vale of tears
　　Where ties are broken, and love is tempest driven—
You'll love me as fondly as I have e'er loved you,
　　In the unchanging light of an eternal heaven.

————

　　"Farewell"—that word we all must speak,
　　How it wearies the heart and fades the cheek.

SING ON, GENTLE MUSE.

Sing on, gentle muse, you shall be heard again!
Your soft notes shall float upon the breeze
      To comfort the outcast and the poor;
From the lone meadows to the hill-tops drear
Your gentle notes shall charm the savage ear
      That never cared for song before.

Like a light-winged bird you shall ascend
Far above the many jealous tongues
      That seek to wound your lonely heart;
You shall be heard, and while you sing of love,
And soar afar like some lone turtle dove,
      You must receive the critics' dart.

They are many, and very rash indeed,
And often fling their poison'd arrows deep
      Down in the heart's tender'st core;
But the wound they inflict will not be as hard to bear
As that inflicted by the friends you once held dear
      'Round your own fond native door.

MYSTERIOUS TEAR!

From what warm region comest thou,
Oh, thou strange and erring drop,
      So crystal clear?
E'en on the smooth white cheek of youth
Thou dost leave thy lasting stain—
      Mysterious TEAR!

DESTROY IT NOT.

Go shatter the walls of some beautiful city
   That is noted for grandeur and fame,
Rather than cast a suggestive remark
   To destroy a woman's fair name.

The walls of a city can be erected again,
   Their beauty be grander than ever;
But a woman's good name once destroyed
   Can ne'er be reclaim'd, no never.

All Heaven has no water soft enough,
   Nor earth no cleansing soap,
That can wash the crimson from the heart
   That destroys a woman's hope.

ALAS! CAROLINA!

Alas! Carolina! Carolina! Fair land of my birth,
   Thy fame will be wafted from the mountain to the sea
As being the greatest educational centre on earth,
   At the cost of men's blood thro' thy "one X" whiskey.

Two very large elephants* thou hast lately installed,
   Where thy sons and thy daughters are invited to come,
And learn to be physically and mentally strong,
   By the solemn proceeds of thy "innocent" rum.

*Winthrop and Clemson colleges.

THEY LAID HER DOWN IN A LONELY GRAVE.

They laid her down while the autumn leaves were falling,
   In a lonely grave beside the deep blue sea;
Her angel spirit is now beyond recalling,
   And her fair form can ne'er revisit you and me.

They laid her low while the autumn winds were sighing
   Thro' the half-clad trees on yonder lonely hill;
The breeze that passed o'er the grave where she was lying
   Was as soft as the wind that ripples the gentle rill.

She sleeps to-day in all her truth and loveliness,
   The purest and gentlest of her gentle kind ;
We loved her, and loved her none the less
   For the little faults which she has left behind.

Soon summer's morn will brighten her resting place,
   And scatter its dew above her azure eyes;
The little birds will sing 'round her happy face,
   And the flowers bloom sweetly 'neath the sunny skies.

The violet will bloom beside the lily there,
   Bound, as by love, in some sweet magic spell,
And ev'ry petal a brighter hue will wear
   For her who sleeps below—a crushed immortelle.

So let her sleep, in all her gentleness,
   Like some sweet form in love's enchanting dream;
She'll bloom again in all her perfectness,
   The lily of holy love beside a crystal stream.

The sweetest beam of love and grace
Is that which glows on ~~an honest~~ face.

A CRYSTALIZED ROSE.

In my garden I stroll'd on a cold winter morn,
  As the beautiful snow lay under my feet;
The hills and the dales, and all I beheld,
  Was laden and shining with glist'ning sleet.

All 'round me there glitter'd, above and below,
  Icicles in groups and icicles in rows;
I saw at my feet in a mantle of sleet
  The half-blown bud of a beautiful rose.

I gather'd the rose in its glittering robe,
  And tenderly bore it to the warmth of my room,
Where I gazed on its leaves till the ice dripp'd away,
  Then naught I beheld but the sweet-scented bloom.

On my mantle I placed it in a brown-color'd vase
  Where no roses, save summer's, had cluster'd before,
It petals soon open'd and my chamber was sweet
  With its delicate odor for a fortnight or more.

As I thought of this lonely and innocent bud,
  Too modestly blooming for man to behold,
I remember'd the form of a beautiful girl
  Cast out in the world to die in the cold.

As I gazed on its leaves so tender and sweet,
  More perfect than the rose in the morning of May,
I pictured the face of that beautiful being
  Away from the sunlight of life's sweet day.

I thought of her life with its winter and frost,
  And how truly unhappy her moments had been—
I wished I had borne her, like the sweet rose,
  To my chamber of love—and admitted her in.

She budded and bloomed in the garden of sorrow,
    Passed down to her grave in the mould'ring clay;
Her beautiful spirit's now blooming in heaven—
    The snow and the ice have all melted away.

IN REMEMBRANCE.

(Written on the flyleaf of a volume of poems which the author presented to a young lady friend in Nashville, Tenn. Over the verses a red rose was pressed.)

'Tis only a rose which I tenderly plucked,
    And lovingly bore from the garden's dew;
It may not be fair, but it tells of the care
    The poet has displayed in remembrance of you.

Here let it remain tho' wither'd and crushed,
    It tells of a friendship unfading and true;
Tho' on this fair page it leaves but a stain,
    That stain shall be sweet, if in remembrance of you.

WHEN SHE IS GONE.

No truer deed in token of love will I employ,
Than to scatter o'er her lonely resting place
    Fresh immortelles
In fond mem'ry of the life and love
Of that dear old mother who always loved her boy.

Tho' Time's cold hand may steal from me life's dearest joy,
And I be left alone in a wide, wide world,
    Sadly forsaken—
Yet naught can take from me the life, the love,
Of that dear old mother who always loved her boy.

FAREWELL, SWEET HOME!

Farewell, sweet home of my childhood hours!
   Where joy and sorrow were blended;
Within thy halls I have loved and lost,
   But now those scenes are ended.

In other days when hope was dawning new
   In the hearts that gather'd 'round thy hearth,
A loving band had just been gather'd there,
   When one by one they faded to earth.

Farewell, sweet home of my childhood hours!
   Strange hours of joy and pain;
The smiles, the tears, thus mingled there,
   Can ne'er the like be felt again.

MORE CARE FOR THE NECK THAN FOR THE INTELLECT.

Fair lady, on that snowy neck and half-clad bosom
Which you so publicly reveal to man,
   There's not a single outward stain or speck;
Would that you had given but half the care
To the training of your intellect and heart
   As you have given to that spotless neck.

For Time, alas! must touch with cold, unerring hand,
That fair bosom's soft, untarnish'd hue,
   Staining that lily-leaf of your sweet sex;
Then in ignorance you will journey here below,
Hiding that once fair bosom 'neath a veil,
   With a standing collar 'round your wrinkled neck.

"UNSTEADY I STAND."

(On hearing a lady, speaking of her past life and hopes, say: "I am now on the verge of womanhood; eighteen summers' old; but oh, how unsteady I stand!")

"Unsteady I stand" on the very verge
  Of womanhood, and cast aside ;
I cannot retrace life's journey now,
  On its gloomy waters I would not glide.

No bark doth drift on that lone stream
  Whose angry waters below me roll—
My youthful dream of life is o'er,
  I stand alone with troubled soul.

Could I but mount the wind that wings
  Its rapid flight across my way,
Fain would I go—as in a dream—
  And sail thro' lands of endless day.

Could I but float in that lone sound,
  That echo from a world of woe—
I'd close these eyes in endless sleep—
  Careless of where my soul would go.

Could I but climb to yonder skies
  On this golden sunbeam at my feet,
There I would find my home, my heaven,
  Youth's dream fulfill'd and friendship sweet.

———

Alas! strange man! so prone to win some maiden's heart,
  And cause it to swell with grief and pain ;   [bird
Like some school boy seeking to cage and wound the sweet
  Whose life he can never make cheerful again.

OTHER DAYS.

Who does not love when youth is past
To wander back to scenes he loved
   In days gone by;
To sit in some familiar spot
Where the evening sunbeams gather, from
   A cloudless sky.

Who does not love to hear the notes,
The wild notes of the soaring lark,
   High o'er the trees;
To see it soar around his head,
Then softly 'light in the meadow grass,
   In June's sweet breeze.

Who does not love to linger 'round
The sunny spot where he once roved
   A careless boy;
To pluck sweet violets from the bed
On which he plucked them long ago,
   With heart of joy.

FAREWELL, SWEET SUMMER!

Farewell, sweet Summer! my own fair guest,
 You have given this heart no pain;
May brighter joys attend your peaceful visit
 When you come to my bosom again.

You have kissed my cheeks with your rose-tint lips
 As I sat at sweet eve in the lane;
I shall sigh for the touch of those passionate lips
 Till you come to my bosom again.

FAREWELL, LILIAN!

Farewell Lilian! you are going
  Far away to leave me now;
You shall be the sunlight, Lilian,
  That shall linger on my brow.

Fate hath whisper'd, you must leave me,
  And you cannot well delay;
We must part, perhaps forever,
  On this balmy autumn day.

Would that I had never met you,
  Never held your gentle hand,
Then my heart had ne'er been broken,
  To sorrow in its native land.

Would that I had never loved you,
  Never press'd your lips to mine;
Then I would to-day be happier,
  Bowing at some nobler shrine.

Yet the love which you have taught me
  Ne'er shall fade within my breast,
But shall beam along my journey
  Like a sunbeam from the west.

If when you are lonely, Lilian,
  You should bear a smile for me;
Let that smile be as the sunlight
  On a dark and troubl'd sea—

For my life is like its billows,
  Dark and gloomy as the night;
Save when you are shedding on me
  Your sweet ray of morning light.

Farewell, Lilian! if forever
  We should thus be borne apart,
Think of me, and love me as kindly
  As I have loved your gentle heart.

———

SHE FELL LIKE A FLAKE OF SNOW.

She was beautiful once ; but she fell
  To the clay-stained earth below ;
Her tender form came down to die,
  As softly as a flake of snow.

She was beautiful once ; but she fell
  To the lowest depth of woe ;
She can never be spotless again,
  And as pure as a flake of snow.

She was beautiful once ; but she fell,
  And some said, "let her go."   *How heartless*
For she can never shine again
  Like a beautiful flake of snow.

She was beautiful once ; but she fell
  Just three sad years ago ;
She fell in the grave of sorrow,
  And lay like a flake of snow.

She was beautiful once; but she fell,
  Ne'er to rise again, ah, no;
She fell in all her loveliness,
  And vanish'd like a flake of snow.

KEEP SILENT, HAND!

Weak hand of mine, keep silent ever,
If this bosom beats apart
  From all that is good and true;
Pen not a line that would lead to vice,
For what is written on this scroll
  Eternity can not undo.

Keep silent, hand! for the gift to tell
The thoughts that linger in this heart
  Was not by mankind given;
And I must suffer in the end
For ev'ry word I hereon trace
  That would keep a soul from heaven.

———

SO-CALLED FRIENDSHIP.

We call it "Friendship," yet how strange
  It moves in this cold world of ours;
It may be just, it may be true,
  But it does n't live in nature's bowers.

'Tis but a kind of unknown being,
  Roaming in the highest spheres—
If you grasp it, 'twill deceive you
  By the holy garb it often wears.

It is no spirit from the heavens,
  Nor the regions of the dead;
But a kind of unknown demon
  Manufactured in the head.

PRETTY MISS LOU.

You may speak of the lily in all its splendor,
  And the dear little violet with its leaves of blue ;
These may be lovely, but they cannot be compar'd
  To the sweet, gentle face of my charming Miss Lou.

You may dream of your visit to the garden of love
  Where your heart 'mid its rapture beat never untrue;
This may be the brightest fair dream of your life,
  But mine is far brighter when I think of Miss Lou.

You may smile at the mem'ry of those rose-tint cheeks
  That once press'd your bosom with a pressure too true ;
That mem'ry may be sweet, but to me there is none
  So dear as the mem'ry of my pretty Miss Lou.

You may dote on that love that too often is shaken,
  And may treasure the ties which Time may undo ;
But the love that is constant, and the ties that are firm,
  I could find, if she'd let me, in my gentle Miss Lou.

As I roam in life's garden of sweet-scented flowers,
  For no tenderer bud from its gems will I sue
Than this sweet little jonquil that's blooming alone,
  And it is none other than my charming Miss Lou.

————

If you mean for me not to love you, sweet May,
  You must turn those dark blue eyes away,
And let me not see them, or else I will sue
  For no love save yours, while looking on you.

I WISH I WAS THERE.

I wish I was by that rippling stream
Where oft I roamed in boyhood days
   When my heart was young and gay,
And my footsteps light and swift
As the wild deer's for some quiet brook
   By a green hill far away.

I wish I was nigh that mossy cliff
From whose summit I've watched the sun
   At the close of day depart,
As a single ray from its golden beam
Would kiss my cheek, then fade away,
   As love-light fades from the heart.

I wish I was where I once have been,
When the bloom of youth was on my cheek,
   And hope was in this breast;
When the tide of life was warm with truth,
And gentle love was utmost there,
   And all was peace and rest.

I wish I was young and had no CARE
To draw this breast adown to earth,
   And fill these eyes with tears;
And the lily-hand of love and peace
Had the same sweet touch as in other days,
   How few would be my fears.

I wish I was nigh that angel face
That shone in early days so fair—
   My bright and morning star—
Whose downy cheeks that so oft have press'd
This bosom—have left an impress there
   Eternity can never mar.

THE WORKING GIRL.

Sweet working girl—as thou dost pass along the street,
　Pursuing thy humble, honest toil,
Cursed be he who would dare to cast a slur
　On thee—thy virtuous name to spoil.

Sweet working girl—I love to view the happy smiles
　On thy fair and ever-beaming face—
Thy perfect form, tho' devoid of rich apparel,
　Is lovelier far because of its simple grace.

Sweet working girl; tho' thy earthly lot seem hard,
　And faint be the hope within thy breast,
Yet thou art blest, for thro' thy faithfulness
　Thou wilt gain Heaven's eternal rest.

Sweet working girl—tho' false stars shine around thee
　While thy cheeks with CARE grow pale,
Take courage then, for there's a morning star that glows
　For thee—behind life's gloomy veil.

Sweet working girl—tho' Fate has destined thy fair hand
　To labor in place of a wayward brother,
Yet Heaven will reward thee for thy honest toil
　In support of thy aged, widow'd mother.

A GLOOMY PICTURE.

From early youth to the frost of age
　Man's days have been a mixture
Of all that constitutes in life
　A dark and gloomy picture.

TO LAURA.

Ah, Laura, when you roam in dreams of solitude,
  And your smiles grow sad as dying sunbeams on the sea,
Will you not, 'mid those hours of loneliness,
  Gaze oft on these true lines and sometimes think of me.

Will you not, at night when those bright eyes are closed
  In dreams, and you recall sweet moments past and gone,
Think of me—and from some pleasant thought may you
  Learn to love me on the beautiful rising morn.

Sweet Laura, I love the sunlight on your crimson cheeks,
  And the gleam of hope that lingers 'round your placid brow;
I love them, and in my life's most dreary hours
  They shall remain to me as dear as they are now.

Fond Laura, if e'er your loving breast shall feel
  Lonely and forsaken by the friends you once held dear,
Think of me, as one who loves you truly well,
  Though I in your fond heart may have no share.

———

THE MIND.

The mind that cannot create worlds,
  Make hills and mountains great and small,
And streams and lakes, and thus the like,
  Is to my mind—no MIND at all.

And people, too, it should create,
  Of ev'ry class, the rich and poor—
Woman should be made queen of all—
  Beautiful—then nothing more.

MAUD, THE MILL, AND THE LILY.

I hate the winding path that leads
  Adown the shadowy glen;
I can view the scenes I never loved
  More vividly now than then.

There is the same familiar stream,
  Whose waters I oft have drank,
And the old mill pond, from whose dark edge
  I oft, so oft have shrank.

The old mill house is standing still
  Where the neighbors ground their corn ;
The night-owl sleeps beneath its roof
  When the nightly shades are gone.

Fast to the door-post and the roof
  The melancholy ivy cleaves,
While high above the gentle winds
  Sigh thro' the lonely forest leaves.

Thro' the cracks of the old flood-gate
  The blackish waters flow,
Dashing, foaming, mingling with
  The angry stream below.

I hate the roaring, chilly sound,
  That so oft did greet my ear,
Of the solemn waters, flowing still
  Below the mill house drear.

Beside those waters once there sat
  A being clothed in white,
With slender form and lily-hand,
  And countenance pure and bright.

Maud—for her gentle name was Maud—
  Wore many smiles, and they were sad;
A thousand virtues she retained,
  Many of which I never had.

Her raven locks were silken soft,
  Dark and bright her sparkling eyes;
Her face was like the summer sun
  Glowing in the eastern skies.

While the old mill wheel shriek'd and roar'd
  Maud would often watch and wait
And list to the foaming waters pass
  Below the old flood-gate.

'Twas in sweet May, as the sinking sun
  Was shedding o'er the hills a gleam,
Maud, who loved the woodland flowers,
  Wander'd down beside the stream.

The evening shades soon gather'd 'round,
  And darkness hover'd o'er her path;
No sound did greet her lonely ear
  Save the night-owl's fickle laugh.

Dark clouds arose and slowly passed,
  Hiding the stars above her head—
She wander'd by the lonely stream
  Like some sweet spirit 'round the dead.

Maud did not heed the roaring sound
  Of distant thunder in the west,
Nor did she fear the lightning's flash
  Glist'ning on her snowy breast.

Beside those waters once there sat
   A being clothed in white,
With slender form and lily-hand,
   And countenance pure and bright.

The wind arose, the thunder roar'd,
  The forest trees fell with a crash;
No living thing could there be seen
  Save little Maud in the lightning's flash.

What a lovely view for angels' eyes
  To have looked upon that gentle form
Clad in white, and slowly moving
  In the dark, terrific storm.

Close by the stream on a grassy mound
  A tender lily waved in sight—
The silvery lightning from the clouds
  Had revealed to Maud its petals white.

She stroll'd toward the lily fair,
  As one would stroll within a dream
To find the angel-form they loved
  And lost—beyond life's sullen stream.

Maud's gentle feet had stray'd too near
  The darkish streamlet's mossy bank—
She stooped and plucked the lily fair,
  But both beneath the waters sank.

Oh, Maud! how oft have I, too, stroll'd
  Beside those waters at your side;
How often have I, too, revealed
  To you the love I could not hide.

How often have I gazed into
  Your dark and ever-beaming eyes;
While gazing there have I not felt
  My bosom freed from mortal sighs?

Have I not press'd your lily-hand,
    And blushing cheek unto this breast;
In the stillness of that happy hour
    Have I not felt the sweetest rest?

Have I not with the gentlest touch
    Unbraided your locks of silken hair,
And turning your dove-like face to mine,
    Have I not call'd you my angel fair?

I hate the lily, hate the stream,
    That solemn flow of angry waters,
But, oh, how sweet to think of Maud,
    The fairest of the miller's daughters.

I hate the path that leads adown
    Beside the lone and dreary mill—
The shadows of that blackish pond
    Are painful to my memory still.

———

HOW STRANGELY DARK.

Her dark eyes—I wou'd that they were not like mine,
            So strangely dark;
I would that they had less of human passion's
            Deep burning spark.

I dare not—e'en when bidding her adieu,
            Hold her warm hand;
For there would come a spark from her bright eyes
            I couldn't withstand.

AN OUTCAST PEARL.

Down in the heart of that newly open'd bud,
Tried by the wind of many a troubled gale,
   Lies the destiny of a being young and fair;
The peace and joy that might have reigned within
That tender heart that never dreamed of sin,
   Are gone, alas! forever buried there.

So kind and gentle she grew into her teens
(Close beside the dingy rose of baffled love)
   Too purely beautiful for earthly care—
Her heart was young—too innocent and young
To dream of the shame a fallen mother brings
   On the child she once held tenderly and dear.

In girlhood days she'd seen the deeds of vice
That blight the home where happiness would reign,
   And cloud the sunlight on its grassy lawn—
She'd lived, she'd loved—and yet she had not lived
Since life's fond hopes had faded in her breast—
   To live without hope one had better ne'er been born.

'Twas faultless love which heaven bade her bear
For her upon whose bosom she'd slept in infancy,
   Unconscious of her lone, mysterious birth—
The stain of that mother's sin which she in after years
Must e'er endure, had made her nothing else
   Than an outcast pearl in the miry slums of earth.

An outcast pearl!—but what else could that angel be
In this condemning world of sin and strife,
   Tho' her heart be as pure as the highest flakes of snow?—
She was tempted and tried, but never did she sin,
Tho' borne on the hard and ever-cruel breast
   Of one whose highest aim was all that was mean and low.

Along thro' life she'd watched the downward course
Of her whose guilty sins she too must bear,
   Unable, alas! to change or rectify that course—
She'd prayed from early youth till girlhood days
For deeds that might not stain her life in after years,
   But, alas! she could not close that fountain's hellish
     source.

Why should she be born within a world like this,
Where a pure girl is forever cast aside
   If she cannot boast of her parents' virtuous name,
While the sin-stained heart is honor'd and beloved
Because of the garb of righteousness it wears
   To shield from human eyes its misery and shame.

Ofttimes she sat on her lonely porch at eve
As the golden sunbeams kissed her gentle feet,
   On the solemn verge of each departing day;
She watch'd those beams till they withdrew their gold,
And thought how sweet if she could only go
   With those soft beams, and forever fade away.

The shadows that gather'd 'round her humble home
Were darken'd, alas! by the breath of human scorn,
   Yet heaven's sunbeams delighted to kiss her feet,
And leave their peace upon her lonely brow,
And their fond hope within her weary heart,
   These latter gifts to her were most divinely sweet.

To-day she stands in all her tenderness,
Alone, forsaken by mankind and her sex,
   A pearl too pure to grace an angel's breast—
She must live, then die, and then be laid away
In some lone spot—perhaps a desert field—
   And then her pure, angelic spirit will be at rest.

No human form will stand beside that lonely grave
When she is gone, and shed a sympathizing tear
   For her who sleeps in true forgetfulness ;
Kind Nature will waft o'er her its gentle breeze
And plant sweet violets 'round her sinless head—
   For Nature loved her more—humankind the less.

————

YOU'LL NEVER SEE IT.

(On being asked by a young lady, just after a renowned Northern
journal had given my works a page of complimentary review, if my hat
was not "too small for my head.")

You'll never see this head too large for my hat,
   You may watch it and feel it as oft as you choose;
But you'll learn, as millions of people have learned,
   Of my character and name thro' my innocent muse.

what a vast audience!

You'll never see this form clad in gaudy apparel,
   Nor these feet playing the "dude" in patent-leather shoes;
But your childrens' children will some day read
   Some pleasant quotations from my innocent muse

How prophetic! 1930—

————

DEVOTION.

I know a white hand that will place
A bunch of violets o'er this face
   When I am gone—
Sweet violets from beneath the bowers
Where I have spent my happiest hours
   In life's sweet morn.

HOPE, SWEET HOPE!

Oh, Hope, sweet Hope! resplendent ray!
Thou hast promised this heart a brighter day,
      A day of joy and peace ;
For me thou hast upon thy gilded beam
The sunlight of a happier dream
        Ere my days shall cease.

Oh, Hope, sweet Hope! why longer wait?
Soon youth is past, and 'tis too late
      For the boon for which I sigh ;
The glow of dark eyes will be dim,
Encircled by ill-health's darken'd rim,
       And smiles grow cold and die.

Oh, Hope, sweet Hope! this weary breast
Fain would call on thee for rest
      From ev'ry inmost care;
Earth's joy and peace can ne'er be mine
While that resplendent ray of thine
       Brings no fond object near.

Oh, Hope, sweet Hope! to thee I bow,
I've waited long, am waiting now
      To realize thy bliss;
Soon in the grave this form shall lie,
Mould'ring 'neath yon star-lit sky—
       Dead to thy raptur'd kiss.

I have promised her ne'er to mention her sweet name again;
But, oh, how the fulfillment of that promise gives me pain.

THE MIDNIGHT HOUR.

'Tis midnight—that most solemn hour in life,
When stern Nature, growing weary with stillness,
Lays her head upon the lap of Almighty God;
And there without a troubled dream she lies,
Breathing as an infant on its mother's breast,
While poor mankind must sleep the sleep of death.

The sleep of death!—For what is that dread hour
To the human soul but an hour of conscious pain
Borne by the vision of a mysterious realm?
A realm beyond the grave where all must tend
To gather with the countless millions that have pass'd
Along that journey—in happiness or woe.

'Tis the hour when ev'ry human heart must learn
What it hath gained in life, and what it costs to die
With an account unbalanced for eternity—
When the last fond ray of hope must fade away
As a golden sunbeam behind the western clouds,
Leaving the human soul in shadows dark to roam.

'Tis midnight—when we awake—if awake we must,
In tears—to think of those we've early loved
And lost, and whose fond memory brings
The dawn of other sunny days around us
When spring-tide's roses bloom'd beside our path,
Only to fade in the hour of midnight gloom.

'Tis the hour when life's star flickers low
On the verge of death's descending cloud,
Behind whose summit there may be peace
And a silvery lining for us, poor mankind,
Whose life, ambition, all, are center'd in the hope
Of some eternal star beyond this vale of tears.

"THROUGH STORM ON EARTH TO PEACE
IN HEAVEN."

The following lines were suggested on seeing a very sad and beautiful
picture in a magazine not long since, entitled: "Through Storm on
Earth to Peace in Heaven."

On a tumultuous sea, dashed by the waves is a frail little bark, rowed
by an aged Prophet. Lying on two beams across the boat is a bier on
which lies the lifeless form of a beautiful young girl, with hands crossed
on her bosom, and face turned slightly to one side. Bending o'er this
fair figure, as if in the act of imparting a farewell kiss, is the weeping
mother. On the bosom of the departed one lies a wreath of fresh
immortelles. White roses lie upon her feet.

.Beneath the dark and gloomy clouds
　　The little bark is tempest driven,
See it ride upon the billows
　　"Thro' storm on earth to peace in heaven."

See the brave old Prophet standing
　　With shining oar in faithful hand,
Battling 'gainst the raging tempest
　　Thro' earthly storm to a sunny land.

See the mother bending lowly
　　O'er the cold and lifeless form
Of her fair and sinless child,
　　Passing thro' life's beating storm.

See the foaming billows dashing
　　Almost o'er the slender bark
As it floats within the tempest
　　On the waters lone and dark.

But the Prophet steers it onward,
   Tho' its beam be almost riven,
To that fair, eternal shore,
   Beyond life's storm to peace in heaven.

Hear him speak to the weeping mother,
   In whose heart is grief and pain—
"Have faith, and you shall soon be where
   Your precious child will live again."

"Many a spotless soul I've rowed
   O'er these waters lone and dark;
But a PURER form I ne'er have borne
   Than she who sleeps in this lone bark."

Hear the mother faintly whisper,
   As darker grows the chilly night,
"Oh, Prophet, Saviour, tell me when
   I shall see just a ray of light?"

"Have faith," the Prophet firmly spoke,
   "And soon you'll reach the eternal shore,
Where your loved-one will be happy,
   And at sweet rest forever-more."

Thro' the darkness peers the mother,
   As the Prophet rows them on—
"Oh," she says, "I see the sunlight
   Of a fair and glorious morn!"

Soon they reach that shining harbor
   Where mortal sins are all forgiven—
She passed, as I and you must pass,
   "Thro' storm on earth to peace in Heaven."

HAIL, THOU QUEEN!—ATLANTA!

(Written during the Exposition.)

Queen of the South! arrayed in white,
    All eyes are now upon thee
O'er this great nation, far and wide,
    And across the dark blue sea.

Men and maidens flock to thee,
    Like birds unto a sunny clime,
To feel thy warmth and view thy grace,
    And hear thy gay bells sweetly chime.

Upon thy breast a wreath of lilies
    Adorn thy being, rich and fair;
The rose of many a sunny land
    Clusters in thy golden hair.

Hail thou Queen! whose gentle hand
    Bears no trace of gloomy fetters;
Upon thy faithful heart is graven,
    "Welcome," in golden letters.

Thy feet are firm, and shall endure
    To reach ambition's lofty height;
Thine arm is love, and must prevail
    To lead from darkness into light.

Hail, thou Queen of Southern beauty!
    Decked with jewels rich and rare;
Wisdom, honor, love, ambition,
    Dwell beneath thy golden hair.

CAN YOU BLAME ME?

We have looked on each other too oft in this life—
  Your smiles from my eyes were not hid—
Can you blame me for loving your matchless face
  As fondly and dearly as I did ?

The memory of your dark blue, passionate eyes,
  Oh, say, can I ever get rid
Of that heavenly dream, and the sunlight of love,
  That so tenderly shown from each lid.

From that streamlet of love in your beautiful heart
  How sweet if my soul could but drink,
And bathe 'mid the lilies in its crystal waters,
  And rest on its moss-cover'd brink.

HOW SWEET.

How sweet when our lonely soul grows weary,
  And our tired feet need rest,
To recline 'neath the shade of the willow tree,
  Pillow'd on a maiden's breast.

To feel a passion pure within us,
  And not the one that seeks to rob
That beautiful virtue underlying
  Her peaceful bosom's honest throb.

To know you can withstand temptation,
  And cause no pang of pain and grief
To wound that breast resigned to you,
  As spotless as the lily's leaf.

FEW WOULD RETURN.

Few are they that have journey'd here below
  Who have not seen their brightest hopes decay—
That would retrace their steps from youth to age,
  And see again those fond hopes pass away.

Few are they that would return in life,
  No matter how bright their journey may have been,
And travel the same old familiar path,
  And view and love again what they could never win.

Few are they that would consent to go
  Back to the shrine where they knelt in other days,
And loved and lost, and spent their after years
  In the mem'ry of some harp-string's plaintive lays.

Few are they that would tread the rugged path
  That leads adown the valley of grief and care,
And see again what their own eyes have seen,
  And shed, alas! the same embitter'd tear.

Few are they that would retrace life's path,
  No matter how bright its sun or sweet its dew—
The hand of love would be a wither'd hand,
  And the bosom of truth would beat, alas! untrue.

———

I'D RATHER OWN HER LOVE.

I'd rather own the love of that modest little maiden
  Who lives in a lonely cottage between two gentle rills,
Than to win the greatest fame all this world can give,
  Or own the fatted cattle on a thousand grassy hills.

I DISLIKE A VAIN AND HAUGHTY MAN.

If I must rise by haughty steps
  To the golden heights that lead to fame,
Then I prefer to remain below,
  Behind an humble, Christian name.

I dislike a vain and haughty man,
  However bright his future may be;
He must lie down within the dust,
  And lay aside his vanity.

I'm sorry for that mortal man
  Who treads upon God's holy clay,
Too vain to lend a helping hand
  To one that has fallen by the way.

If I should rise to lofty heights,
  An humble heart shall be thereon;
And tho' you may be far below,
  Remember, you I shall not scorn.

For what tho' I obtain the praise
  Of human lips both far and wide,
A worm of dust I still must be,
  Drifting on life's gloomy tide.

LIVE HONEST; BE KIND.

Much thought and the pen will accomplish all things,
  You must think and be wise in the thought you pursue—
Live honest, be kind, and you'll surely succeed,
  And the world be made brighter by having known you.

THE DAYS OF MY YOUTH.

(On re-visiting the home of my boyhood.)

Would that the friends I loved in youth
    Were close beside me here to-day,
On this loved spot where we once played
    When our hearts were young and gay.

How sweet would be each moment now,
    If I but only once again
Could form the self-same group beside
    These violets in the lane.

'Round this hallow'd spot there float
    Sweet memories of the past,
Of dear associations gone—
    They were too fond to last.

'Twas 'neath this drooping willow tree
    I sat alone—without a name*—
At school with nature's God to learn
    The hidden path that leads to fame.

'Twas here I linger'd in the twilight
    With no teacher at my knee
Save kind Nature with her flowers,
    And a bosom full and free.

Full and free with radiant hope
    Like a ray of glorious light,
Pointing this young and tender heart
    To the path of Truth and Right.

* The author never was named in childhood by his parents, but was
left the pleasure of selecting his given-name at the age of fourteen.

'Twas here I learned that solemn truth
  That the life to pleasure given
Will never reach its shining goal
  On this bright side of heaven.

Each violet as it bloomed beside
  My humble feet in morning dew,
Taught me that the purest, noblest life,
  Must be begun when hope is new.

ON THE DEATH OF EDGAR W. NYE.

How strange is Nature! and the workings
    Of the great invisible God
        Whose doings are just and right;
Who preserves the spark that ne'er can glow
    The dullest of humankind—
        Yet quenches the brightest light.

How strange, indeed, and wondrous wise
    Must be that gracious Hand
        Whose works we can ne'er undo,
That it should spare the dull, illiterate mind
    Rather than the flame of genius
        Is alas! too sadly true.

Can it be Death?—Shall we not hear again
    In eternity—some where—
        The voice of him who once spake
To cheer the gloomy lives of humankind?
    Bringing joy and gladness
        To hearts that fain would break.

UNFORGIVEN—ADIEU!

Good-by!—another sun is sinking,
  Shedding its golden beams about
       Our youthful feet—
I stand 'neath the canopy of heaven
Close by your side, but unforgiven
       By your lips sweet.

'Tis true I may have caused you pain,
  And your sweet eyes sometimes a tear
       To dim their hue;
But you, in youth's sweet bloom I trust
Will not esteem me e'er unjust—
       My heart untrue.

For I, as sure as yonder sun
  Scatters its crimson on your cheeks,
       Have loved your heart ;
Have shielded you amid life's fears,
Helped you to dry your bitterest tears—
       Yet we must part!

Can you, as mem'ry calls you back
  To the happy moments we've spent upon
       Yon dewy hill,
Now deem this heart too false and low
To be looked upon, save as a foe
       You'd gladly kill?

Twas there, amid the dew of heaven,
  I held your gentle hand too oft
       To deem you false;
I've always found you pure and chaste ;
Man's arms have ne'er entwined your waist—
       You did not "waltz."

UNFORGIVEN—ADIEU!

But still you unforgiving stand,
Turning from me those gentle eyes,
So sweet and true.

But still you unforgiving stand,
　Turning from me those gentle eyes,
　　So sweet and true;
You have suggested that we should part,
Then here's my hand—you have my heart—
　　Good-by! adieu!

CHRIST ON CALVARY.

See him as he hangs beside the guilty thieves,
　Reviled, condemn'd, and forever cast aside;
See him as he views his well-beloved friends,
　Thirsting for the blood of his own precious side.

See his hands thro' which the nails were driven,
　The accursed nails by an unrelenting Jew;
Hear his voice, as he views the cruel throng:
　"Father forgive them, for they know not what they do."

See the sharp spear as it glistens in the light
　Of the self-same sun that shines on you and me;
See it pierce his pure and spotless side,
　Hear the warm blood as it trickles down the tree.

Hear him as he groans in agony and pain
　As he views his friends in the condemning throng;
Those who cast green palms beneath his feet
　As down to Jerusalem he passed along.

See him as he hangs, a pure and sinless soul,
　Rejected, accursed—for many an oath was hurl'd
On him who died on Calvary's tree
　To redeem forever a sin cursed world.

WHEN WE WERE YOUNG.

Oh, lovely form, begirt in life's resplendent morn
    With flowers too pure to bloom around my wayward feet,
I look on thee, only to repeat those fitting vows
    I oft have vowed—that we no more should meet.

Upon yon hill—if thou'll consent to there retrace
    Our footsteps made in the sands of other years—
I'll carry thee back, away across yon sparkling rill
    To the lonely heights where we shed our first sad tears.

The dew is there—upon the grass leaves hang the drops,
    And the flowers have drank thereof till they are sweet—
'Twill but remind us of those moments long since gone,
    When the same sweet drops once cooled our burning feet.

When we were young, and the first sweet beam of hope
    Glowed warm and true within each peaceful breast,
And love supreme was an ever-present guest,
    Save in that still hour when passion broke our rest.

Oh, why was that burning spirit lingering there,
    Melting our hearts into one imperfect heart ?
And bearing that bliss which sin too often bears
    To hearts that are as one, and cannot beat apart.

IN ATLANTA

    Let me rest 'mid the atmosphere I love,
        And my last repose will be sweet, serene;
    I love that beautiful love that lives
        For one whom the eyes have never seen.

TO ONE WHO IS ALL LOVELINESS.

From thy eyes, as from the sunlight beaming
   O'er the distant hills tinged with autumn's hue,
I catch the gleam of love so long enticing
   My very soul into a haven sweet and new.

Sweet and new—a home of tenderness,
   'Round whose shrine no shadows ever rest;
But love supreme in all its gentleness
   Fills the sweet chamber of thy snowy breast.

I love the sunlight 'round thy placid brow,
   And the smiles that linger on each dimpled cheek;
They draw me up, as sunbeams draw the flower,
   And make me strong when I am truly weak.

I love thy hand, so firm in truthfulness,
   So kind and gentle in its every sphere—
To know thy bosom is all constancy,
   While mine's so fickle—is more than I can bear.

Had thy fair face been veiled before mine eyes,
   And only thy faint voice my ears did greet;
Then I had learned what now I truly know,
   That thou art all LOVE, and gentleness complete.

————

FAREWELL! FOR A TIME.

Farewell, sweet Muse! my dearest companion,
   Thou hast given this heart no feeling of pain;
Some day, ere the setting of life's purple sun,
   When my pathway is brighter, I'll recall thee again.

FAREWELL, SWEET COLLEGE GIRL!

Farewell, ye milk-white dove, farewell!
  This parting gives me pain;
To think, perhaps, I ne'er shall see
  Thy gentle form again.

Farewell!—but thy sweet blooming face,
  Fresh as the dewy morn,
Will leave its impress on this heart
  Long after thou art gone.

Farewell! and if e'er thine azure eyes
  Shall feel the dint of care,
Look up to Him whose loving hand
  Will dry each bitter tear.

Farewell, ye milk-white dove, farewell!
  If on earth we meet no more,
May in that snow-white throng of love
  We meet on yonder shore.

———

MARRIAGE AND DEATH.

Marriage and death—these great events in life,
  Alas! with each other are blended;
A festive scene and a funeral march,
  And man's brief journey is ended.

A marriage puff, and a funeral notice
  Is the end of his transient tale,
And he vanishes from human sight
  Beyond life's dark and gloomy veil.

SIDE BY SIDE, SOME DAY.

You may laugh at affliction,
And shun the poor wretch
   As he drags along life's rugged way;
But remember, your feet
Now nimble and strong,
   May be wither'd and weary some day.

You may spurn the poor wretch
Whose garments are torn,
   But whose heart may be honest and true;
Yet think of this well,
As sure as you live
   Some affliction will fall upon you.

Should he come to your chamber
On a cold winter night
   You would surely turn him away;
Little thinking that you
Must sleep by his side
   Some day in the mouldering clay.

SHE'S ILL.

This Christmas, with all its mirth and joy,
   Will not be enjoyed by me,
For the one whom I love is ill at her home
   On the banks of the Congaree.

How could I join in the circle of pleasure,
   Tho' ever-so enticing it be,
While my dear little lady lies ill at her home
   On the banks of the Congaree.

I CANNOT THINK THAT I'LL BE LOST FOREVER.

I cannot think that I'll be lost forever
    For the little sins that swell this human breast
While in this transitory life
    Where I have never had a day of peace and rest.

I cannot think that in this cloudy world
    Where I exist 'mid its many, many cares,
That after death I'll be borne away
    By an unforgiving hand that wipes away no tears.

I cannot think that in this world of sin
    Where I was forced without my own consent,
That I'll be doom'd to hell at last,
    Without a second chance to e'er repent.

TO AMY.

I will drink to your health, sweet Amy,
    For there's nothing in this cup, I fear,
That would be suggestive of sorrow
    For my own sweet Amy, dear.

May your heart be pure and noble,
    And your arm be firm and strong,
And your hope be like the rainbow,
    Beautiful, bright and long.

May your life, like the rose of summer,
    Be fresh, and remain in its bud,
As I never was partial to whiskey, Amy,
    I'll toast you in Congaree mud.

(FOURTH VOLUME.)

———

SOUTH CAROLINA.

Thou fond home of our early childhood days,
  On thy loved soil we've spent our happiest hours;
We've basked in the beams of thy noon-tide sun,
  And have sat in the shade of thy sweet bowers.

Upon thy hills, in youth and manhood years,
  We've bathed in the dew of thy resplendent morn;
The flowers that bloom'd beside our youthful feet
  To mem'ry have grown sweeter—none are gone.

Beside thy streams we've caught the pleasant sound
  Of rippling waters, flowing onward to the sea—
The most familiar, on which we fain would dwell,
  Is thy fair stream, the beautiful Congaree.

In thy green fields, from early morn till eve,
  We've seen the ploughman till thy fertile soil—
When the autumn leaves 'round his path were strewn
  We've seen him gather the fruit of his honest toil.

In thy cool meadows we've heard the happy notes
  Of sweet birds mingled with the pleasant sound
Of the distant bells of the approaching herd,
  Whose nimble footsteps were heard upon the ground.

On thy sweet lawns we've viewed the perfect form
  Of the angel who sat beneath thy shady trees,
Fairer than the blushing rose of early spring,
  Made lovelier by thy pure and balmy breeze.

'Round thy hearth, beside thy happy shrine,
  We've bowed, but have shed no guilty tear
The life we've spent upon thy peaceful soil
  Has been too calm to e'en suspicion fear.

TO THE YOUNG UNJUST CRITIC.

Challenge me to fight on the open field,
  And hurl at my head the fiery dart,
Rather than belittle the gentle muse
  That issues from this lonely heart.

defiant

Young man—you who never aspired
  To soar no higher than where you are—
As no ambition burns within you,
  Try not to extinguish another's star.

In you there may much genius be—
  A gift that often leads to fame
If used aright—but you are dead
  To that true sense which makes a name.

If you in your self-wisdom feel
  Constrained to criticise my muse,
Let it be JUST, and then you may
  Just criticise it when you choose.

———

COLUMBIA.

Beautiful city, with thy cool, shady groves,
  And picturesque hills, and sweet-scented bowers,
Where the sweet dews of heaven in the stillness of morn
  Refresh the pure lips of thy innocent flowers.

'Round thy houses and lawns there's a sunbeam of love,
  And a gleam of sweet peace encircles thy walls;
True Friendship and Love is the motto that hangs
  O'er the broad-open'd door to thy peace-laden halls.

WE PART TO-NIGHT.

We part to-night—perhaps it may be well
To sever the tie that bore that magic spell
      Ere my heart grew wild;
We've naught to regret, for we've loved each other
As fondly and dearly as a devoted mother
      For her absent child.

We part in peace—never to meet again
As oft we've met down in the grassy lane
      'Neath fragrant bowers,
Where the dew of heaven, fresh and sweet
As that of love, fell 'round our feet
      In the morning hours.

We shed no tears—for tears can never rise
From a still fount to lonely beaming eyes
      When fond love is gone;
We loved once, and can never love again,
That love has cost us many an aching pain
      Since sweet hope has flown.

We'll meet no more—not in this vale of tears
Where we have spent so many changing years
      Of sunshine and frost;
So let it be—for soon we two shall hide
In the cold tomb—no longer to abide
      Where ve've loved and lost.

THAT ROSE.

  ·So charmingly beautiful,
    Seemingly kind;
  So sweet was that rose
    I wished it was mine.

Sweet! [handwritten annotation]

A VIOLET AND A JONQUIL.

A poor little violet once bloom'd in the morn,
But it fell from the jar, and is faded and gone,
And to-day it lies trodden deep under men's feet,
Its color unnatural, its odor unsweet.

Close by the violet, as if under its care,
Grew a little white jonquil, unconscious of fear;
Its hue was perfect as the leaf of the rose,
And its delicate odor was sweet to the nose.

A twig struck the violet one night in a storm,
Parched and dry—the night was so warm—
And the sweet little jonquil, so pure from its birth,
Was jarred by the twig, and fell to the earth.

So the poor little violet, and the bud by its side,
Fell deep in the slums together and died;
And the old earthen jar sits empty to-day,
The violet and jonquil are strewn by the way.

————

THE PAST.

As I turn and listen to the Past
  I hear the echo sweet and low
Of some dear voice, floating still
  In the festive halls of long ago.

I catch a glimpse of parting scenes,
  Familiar in the days gone by;
The happy face, the winning smile,
  The mem'ry of some pensive eye.

TO MISS MATTIE SUE——

As the summer sunbeams
Peep o'er the distant hills
  On some sweet and lonely brook,
So my weary, longing eyes,
Warm with the dew of love,
  To thee alone do look.

On thy rose-bud cheeks
Girlhood's sweetest smiles
  In brightest hope do beam,
And thy lovely azure eyes
Endear my only hope
  And fondest day-dream.

Of thy plaintive voice
I hear an echo sweet
  Sinking deep into my heart,
And that peaceful echo
Bears the enchanting bliss
  Which death alone can part.

———

THE DECEIVER.

He who lays his body down,
Hopeless for eternity—
  An unbeliever—
Will sooner find a place of rest
Beyond this vale of tears,
  Than the DECEIVER.

I LOVE THY SHADES.

Sweet Solitude—I love to spend each quiet hour
In the lone shades of thy sweet bower
      Beside yon rill,
And gazing, with a blessed regard
On Nature, I commune with God,
      And learn His will.

I love thy shades—'tis there alone I learn
MYSELF—the faintest sparks that in me burn
      Are kindled by thee;
In life's dark cell where sunlight fades
I gather hope from thy sweet shades—
      My soul's set free.

TO A VAIN MORTAL.

Vain mortal of a common clay
  From many sins you may be free,
But that which holds the greatest sway
  Within your life—is vanity.

Some little deed you may have done,
  Or perhaps some simple word or hint
Has placed your common name upon
  Some written page, or in public print.

So, proud you stand with lifted cane,
  Like a wood-cock on a cypress log—
The deed that has made you vain could have
  Been performed by a shepherd dog.

MY LASSIE AND I.

I love the winding path that leads beside the old familiar
    wood,
Where I used to roam with a country lass who wore an
    ancient hood;
Who used to take my little hand within her own with care,
And lead me thro' the meadow hay, speaking words of cheer.

My youthful life had almost passed that sweet and happy
    stage
Where the heart is free from trouble and forgetful of old
    age—
Sweet violets bloom'd beside that path, but none was half so
    fair
As my little lass with rosy cheeks and downy auburn hair.

At evening twilight oft we'd sit and hold each other's hand,
And speak of love but that strange term I could not under-
    stand,
For I was young, as I have said, and she extremely fair—
Both acted like summer doves—a quite familiar pair.

Oft while the moonbeam's silvery rays played 'round our
    careless feet
I'd turn and kiss my lassie's lips so gentle and so sweet—
To kiss that lassie, I'll confess, 'twas then I did not loath,
For I was young and she was fair, so please excuse us both.

A thousand glances I have caught from that sweet lassie's
    eyes,
And half as many times we've kissed beneath the star-lit
    skies;
But now her glances are not mine, for she is far away
Kissing other lips than these, in some sweeter meadow's hay.

THE GRAVE WHERE A WOMAN LIES.

I stood alone at the close of day
As the sunbeam's soft and golden rays
    Lit up the eastern skies,
On a lonely hill by a grassy mound
Long neglected and forgotten—
    The grave where a woman lies.

A woman once sought in early years
For the charms of her matchless face,
    Dark hair and sparkling eyes;
On whose fair cheeks was the rosy tint
Of youth—like the rainbow's placid hues
    Bright'ning the eastern skies.

The peaceful rays of the summer sun
Shone softly 'round her lonely bed
    On each sad close of day—
They seem'd to glow in grander beams
Than those on the shining marble
    Where purer ashes lay.

A lesson of love those sunbeams taught,
Of love impartial, just and true,
    From the Lamb of Calvary,
Who, when called upon to act as judge
Of a woman whom the world condemn'd,
    Said, "Nay, I'll not condemn thee."

Would that these lips that ne'er had spoken
To slander that once most perfect name,
    Could call her back again,
And placing the hand of love in her's
I'd learn how freely Christ forgives
    And cleanses the deepest stain.

BESIDE LIFE'S OCEAN.

As I stand beside life's ocean,
  While the moments pass away,
I can feel my weary feet
  Sinking in the miry clay.

As I gaze upon its billows,
  Dashing, foaming as they roll,
I can almost feel them surging
  O'er my very inmost soul.

Lone and weary I am standing,
  Drenched by ev'ry troubled wave,
Waiting to be dashed forever
  In the cold and silent grave.

Ev'ry billow has its sorrow,
  And its flow of briny tears,
Which were gather'd from my cradle
  To my life's meridian years.

Tho' I stand alone, rejected,
  On its shore, and cast aside,
Yet my hope shall find a haven
  Beyond its dark and gloomy tide.

————

'TIS BETTER IT WAS SILENT.

'Tis better this hand was silent,
  This mind obscure and weak,
Than it should pen a single line
  These lips would dare not speak.

A TREE OF VARIED FRUITS AND BUDS.

(On meeting a very handsome lady whom the author once knew and loved in early years, but at this meeting she was accompanied by two beautiful black-eyed girls, about three and five summers, respectively—her own buds.)

This life's a tree; we sit beneath its branches,
  And view the flowers and fruits we still would gather;
Fruits of varied seasons, and of purest kind,
  Flowers that have bloomed sweetest in wintry weather,

Upon each branch there are many opening buds
  Of every hue to please the human mind,
The luscious fruit of a score or more of years
  We view beside those buds till we are blind.

Alas! how strange that we should thus behold
  The fruit we've loved in other sunny years
Still fair and beautiful, and nursing many buds,
  Some for joy and some for bitter tears.

But yesterday, 'twas mine to view two tender buds
  On this sad tree, on which I'm loath to dwell;
They were blooming beside a pure and early fruit
  Which I fain would have plucked—I loved it so well.

———

WHERE VANITY PUFFS THE HEART.

True love will die in palace halls
  Where vanity puffs the heart,
'Twas only made for nature's walks—
  Her paradise of art.

CONCEITED.

Fair lady, your remarks have caused me to believe
Your heart is all vanity, and beats to deceive;
But for the sympathy I cherish for you,
I'll merely inform you, those remarks are untrue.

Far be it from me, fair one, to intrude,
Or act toward you "too forward and rude" —
Tho' your face has for me a beauty untold,
Yet I'm not anxious that face to behold.

Fair one, your acquaintance has never been sought
By me—not in action, or even in thought,
So if ever those sland'rous words you repeat,
Let it be at your home, and not on the street.

———

THE FIRST RAY OF HOPE.

How sweet is the first bright ray of hope
When youth's sweet bloom is on the cheeks,
    And there's music in the breeze,
And the violet blooms beside the wood,
And the lily waves beneath the bay,
    And the budding heart's at ease.

———

INGRATITUDE.

INGRATITUDE, ah, I hate it,
    I'm loath for a moment to dwell
On a word whose only meaning
    Originated in hell.

THE COMING BARD.

When your life-song shall have ended,
And with grief its echo's blended
    O'er your lone head;
Then will some plaintive notes resound
O'er this cold, unhallow'd ground,
    Your final bed.

Some sweet bard shall then arise
And float his muse unto the skies,
    While angels sing
The anthem of a purer soul
Than yours, whose sentiments unroll
    No sacred thing.

On ev'ry hill-top far and near
He'll sing that sinful hearts might hear
    His sweet refrain;
All men will bow before his face,
Whose winning smiles and perfect grace
    Dispel all pain.

———

AUTUMN.

The lilies and violets have faded and gone,
The hills and the meadows are drear and lone,
    The leaves are falling,
Filling our pathway sure and fast,
Telling our souls, they'll soon be cast
    Beyond recalling.

THE PAST—TURN THE PAGE!

Turn the page!—for grief and disappointment
On its once smooth surface
                    Now appears;
  On its margin are finger prints
Made dingy by the bitter drops
                    Of many tears.

TEARS—that dew on which I would not dwell,
  So strange their inward meaning—
                    So very deep;
I would not dwell upon them now,
  Yet o'er this page I still must bend,
                    And still must weep.

Turn the page!—for between each written line
Remorse, in crimson doth appear
                    In brilliant rays;
Remorse—for 'mid life's changing scenes
My life was spent—I dare not tell—
                    In many ways.

———

ON TO ETERNITY.

As I look around me I see moving
  Slowly and unconsciously
    Thousands of immortal souls
      On to eternity;
The youthful, the gay and beautiful
  Form an innumerable caravan,
    Keeping step by the drum-beat
      Of inexorable Time.

FROM THE PALACE TO THE WOODLAND.

'Tis pleasant to descend from lofty heights
  And view this world as a little child;
To leave the stately palace walls
  And roam within the woodland wild.

To gather sweet violets here and there,
  And view the cows go sauntering down
To quench their thirst at a sparkling stream—
  Away from the busy, noisy town.

To recline upon a grassy mound
  Beside some pure and quiet brook,
And gather wisdom, comfort, peace,
  From the pages of some sacred book.

To feel that you are only mortal,
  A little worm of common clay,
Helpless—waiting, hoping, trusting,
  For a home of brighter day.

To lay aside all sinful passions
  That have made life's journey hard;
To gaze into the open heavens
  And find communion with your God.

THE DUDE.

Young man, of your worth you never can boast,
  To society TRUE you are virtually dead,
Because you have played the dude so long,
  With but little heart and an empty head.

THE LOVER'S RETURN ON A BICYCLE.

ADMITTED, BUT NOT ACCEPTED.

Away down 'neath the Southern pine
Where the jessamine and the ivy twine,
  And violets bloom;
Where no fierce winds, cold and bleak,
Touch the maiden's blushing cheek,
  And there's no gloom.

A dove-like form was seen to float—
Like the white sail of some tiny boat—
  Adown the hill;
Nearer and nearer drew the form,
Like a dove in a summer storm,
  Tossed at will.

A maiden fair soon came in sight
With cheeks aglow and countenance bright,
  And slender form;
Her white hands held the handle bars,
Her eyes were like two lovely stars—
  Cheeks bright and warm.

Adown a steep incline she sped,
The golden tresses on her head
  Fanning the breeze;
Heedless of the danger near,
Her youthful heart knew no fear—
  Beneath the trees.

Her charming steel-horse could not miss
A steep and dangerous precipice

By the river's bank;
Along she flew—a fearful sight—
Like a bird wounded in its flight
    She downward sank.

Many an anxious eye drew near,
And gazing with a sense of fear,
        Looked here and there;
No wounded form could there be found,
Nor trace of blood seen on the ground,
        Of the maiden fair.

For safe below the rough incline
She passed beneath the Southern pine—
        Her charming wheel
Never faltering, stood it all,
Thus saving her from a fatal fall
        By its perfect steel.

Away beyond she swiftly flew
Thro' grasses wet with summer's dew,
        O'er turf and stone,
Toward a dreary cottage-door,
Whose moss bespoke of inmates poor,
        And very lone.

Soon she reached this home of gloom,
Alighted near its western room—
        Sat down to rest
On an ancient settee, roughly made,
Within the live-oak's gentle shade,
        And soothed her breast.

There in the cool and balmy breeze
That wafted sweetness from the trees
      On hills afar,
She sat alone, like an angel fair,
Thinking of him, her fondest care,
      And constant star.

Toward the house she calmly stroll'd,
As if no one should her behold
      Seeking those walls ;
While gently tapping on the door
Footsteps were heard upon the floor
      Within its halls.

Familiar were those footsteps too,
Whose sound to her had music true—
      Sweet and sublime ;
Confusion seem'd to swell each hall,
As if no visitors called at all—
      At any time.

But soon the ancient cottage door
With rusty hinges, scraped the floor,
      And opened wide ;
Before her fair face bending low
Stood a wreck of that most bitter flow—
      Affection's tide.

For on this strangely ebbing tide
Many a hope sublime hath died
      In the human breast ;
A "moving tomb-stone," cold, defaced,
Is all that shows where love was placed
      Fore'er to rest.

Affection! ah, that transient thing
From which life's lasting troubles spring,
     By love is taught
First to adore, and then to spurn,
Causing the human heart to burn
     With bitter thought.

Love is its mother—'tis her son,
Whose warmth is like the rays of sun,
     Fading, dying;
A season of but fleeting bliss,
A dream of one eternal kiss—
     Hope belieing.

While standing nigh his bended form
She whisper'd words of friendship warm,
     But all in vain;
She press'd his cold hand to her cheek
So warm and pure—he could not speak,
     So deep the pain.

There's always pain in meeting one
Who was once the lovely rising sun,
     Within your heart;
In ev'ry look and ev'ry word
There's a glance retain'd, an echo heard
     You cannot part.

While gazing on her lovely face,
He admired her gentle, winning grace,
     So sweet and pure;
And wonder'd how her angel-hand
Could e'er have broken love's sacred band
     Once firm and sure.

With cheeks aglow and glances warm,
As sunbeams when the summer storm
        Had passed away,
She looked on him, for she had learn'd
To love the heart she oft had spurn'd
        Each fleeting day.

While gazing on her face so sweet,
He invited her to take a seat
        Within the hall ;
Seating himself beside her there
He thought it naught but just and fair
        To tell her all :—

"I loved you once, oh, pretty one,
You were to me the rising sun
        Of perfect bliss ;
My hope was built on nothing more
Than YOURS, whose beam I did adore,
        And loved its kiss."

"That love was true, you knew full well,
Truer than human lips could tell—
        I loved your name ;
To your sweet life I did impart
My hope, my all, my very heart,
        My life, my fame."

"While you were nigh my path was peace,
My joy and bliss seem'd ne'er to cease—
        Sweet rest was mine ;
My hope was like the sunbeam's ray,
My life like an unclouded day,
        Of purest sunshine."

"Your smiles to me were softer far
Than the silvery light of the purest star
  In heaven's skies;
You were my ALL, my guiding light,
Whose glances were my chief delight,
  From holy eyes."

"But since that peace for which I sighed
Has passed away with hope and died
  A death of pain;
Words now from you tend more to break
This heart you never can awake—
  Never again."

"My heart is on an unknown sea,
Far from the love you bore for me—
  My first and last;
Love's gentle tide has ebbed away,
Life has no boon for me to-day,
  Its summer's past."

'Tis strange the human heart should learn
To loath the love that would return
  And seek its breast;
And stranger 'tis that love should seek
Acceptance in that bosom weak
  It robbed of rest.

As she thought of his youthful heart so lone,
She wonder'd if it was like stone,
  So very cold;
She laid her warm hand on his cheek,
He gazed on her; but could not speak—
  All had been told.

She simply said, "Forgive me, dear?
Let all your sorrows, ev'ry care,
      By ME be borne ;
Ne'er again in this weak heart of mine
Will my fond feelings for you decline
      On love's sweet throne.

"I know that I've been in the wrong,
And treated you unkind too long,
      These many years ;
In your past love I'll firmly trust,
That love to me was ne'er unjust,
      Or caused me tears."

His weary hand she gently raised,
And pressing it to her lips, she praised
      His love again ;
She lingered with a painful smile,
Hoping his heart would all the while
      Be free from pain.

He thanked her, bowed his head and wept
O'er the love that had in her bosom slept
      Many a year.
Those tears to her were strange she knew ;
Naught else than love's eternal dew
      Embalm'd in care.

Away from this lone cottage door
She tried to pass, but felt the more
      Like ling'ring there ;
The thought that she fore'er must part

From him her life, her very heart,
  She could not bear.

Fresh from the bosom of her grief
Came bitter tears, but no relief
    From her sad night;
She slowly passed from this lone door,
Mounted her wheel—to return no more—
    And took her flight.

HOW DEEP THE MYSTERY!

If I should ask this silver coin
That lies within my hand to-day,
    "Tell me thy history?"
And it should speak; alas! how strange,
Would each sad word sound in my ear—
    How deep the mystery!

  *   *   *   *   *

Would it not tell the sick'ning truth
Of some fair one in the bloom of youth
    Whom it had led astray?
How it partly paid for the shining band
That bought sweet virtue from the hand
    Now silent 'neath the clay.

Though a stranger, I loved thee,
  Thou wert near to my heart—
I fain would have met thee,
  But I knew we must part.

ON THE BANKS OF THE CONGAREE.

Many a blissful hour I've spent
  'Mid the shade of the willow tree,
Watching the smoothly flowing waters
  Of the beautiful Congaree.

Many a Sabbath hour I've sat
  With little Maud beside my knee,
Gazing o'er the distant hills
  On the banks of the Congaree.

Many a happy smile I've seen
  On her sweet face, so pure and free,
While sitting in the willow's shade
  On the banks of the Congaree.

Many a balmy kiss I've stolen
  From precious lips, too pure for me,
While caressing lovely little Maud
  On the banks of the Congaree.

Many a charming glance I've seen
  I nevermore will see,
While sitting beside my gentle Maud
  On the banks of the Congaree,

But now those blissful days are gone,
  The willow only stands to tell
Of the pleasant hours I once enjoy'd
  With little Maud I loved so well.

For she in youth and beauty died,
  And I shall see her face no more;
She sits by a lovelier river, 'neath
  Some shady palm on the other shore.

ON THE BANKS OF THE CONGAREE.

But now those blissful days are gone,
The willow only stands to tell
Of the pleasant hours I once enjoy'd
With little Maud I loved so well.

THE CAUSE OF ANOTHER'S WOE.

I had rather live a pauper's life,
My name be unrevered,
   And when I die hellward go,
Than to bear the consciousness within me
That I in this life had been
   The cause of another's woe.

What a sick'ning pang that heart must feel
That knows itself a robber
   Of some pure and virtuous name;
Earth's softest water ne'er can cleanse
Its stain—nor Lethe's sparkling stream
   The mem'ry of its shame.

————

A LOVELY WOMAN'S GLANCE.

Long mayest thou gaze upon the stars
   That twinkle in yon azure skies,
But linger not, oh, passionate man,
   Thy gaze in a lovely woman's eyes!

An army of ten thousand foes
   Is easier subdued in their advance
Than the dangerous feeling often borne
   By a lovely woman's melting glance.

————

The heart that's quick to love when young
   Will soon grow cold when youth is past,
For 'mid life's many sterner scenes
   And troubled dreams, love cannot last.

COLD IN DEATH.

(On the death of a bright young lady, a student of the Winthrop Normal College, who came to her death not long since in this city by being run over by an electric car.)

Cross her hands upon her bosom,
  Smooth back her locks of silken hair;
Gently fold the shroud around her,
  Tho' cold in death she's no less fair.

Lay your hand upon her forehead,
  Sweetly she is resting now;
Touch those eyelids, closed to sorrow,
  While sweet peace pervades her brow.

Kiss the lips that bore no evil,
  As pure as lilies on the lawn ;
Kiss the cheeks that blossom'd sweetly
  On each lovely zephyr morn.

Kiss the hands that moved in friendship,
  Stain them with a tear of joy;
Ask that yours—hands less weak—
  May some loving deeds employ.

Kiss the hair that waved in beauty,
  Like hyacinths of sweet perfume;
Place the white rose on her bosom,
  Soon she'll lie in the silent tomb.

'Tis strange that you will always find
  In the poorest spot the brightest pearls,
So a poverty-stricken'd land is good
  For naught but raising pretty girls.

TO HELEN. → (H.-B.-)

(The following poem pleased Helen very much, and it is with her consent I publish it.)

May you pass o'er the sea of life like a bubble,
And ne'er reach the mouth of the river of trouble,
And from the dark clouds that eternally roll,
May some sweet haven shelter your soul.

good

If e'er in the midst of a season of bliss
Your dear lips burn for a passionate kiss,
Think of me then, though I distantly roam,
And reserve me the right till I visit your home.

May the joys of your young life be without measure,
And not always kindled in the halls of pleasure—
Tho' the mem'ry of pleasure seems ever so dear,
After all 'tis but sorrow, and the source of a tear.

When o'er the gay floor of the ball-room you trip,
And champagne and wine you carelessly sip,
Remember, fair Helen, it is after the ball
That you dream of the moments you would not recall.

So, now fond Helen, as I bid you adieu,
I trust your sorrows of life will be few,
And you'll return unto me, like some sweet dove,
And nestle once more on this bosom of love.

The fairest flower has its flaw,
    The greenest leaf its yellow vein,
The brightest eye its faded beam,
    The purest heart a crimson stain.

indicates a true insight into man's erring nature

EULA AND EUNITA, THE TWO ORPHANS.

They grew up side by side in a cottage by the sea,
Where the ivy and the myrtle entwined the cypress tree ;
Where the odor of sweet roses perfumed the stilly air,
And the hyacinth and lily bloomed tenderly and fair.

They played around the self-same hearth, and 'round the
    loving knee
Of a fond and happy mother, now sleeping by the sea—
Eula was as handsome a girl as ever strolled beneath
The stately cypress or the elm 'round her native heath.

Her cheeks were of that velvet hue that charms the passing
    eye,
Her glances like the silvery light of heaven's star-lit sky;
Her golden locks were charming—like a crown of purest
    gold—
Around her snowy neck they waved in an exquisite fold.

Both were bless'd with wealth in girlhood's early years,
They'd felt no disappointment, vicissitudes or cares ;
They mingled with the throng of the high-toned and the
    gay,
To their intellect and beauty men did homage pay.

Eunita wore a darker shade of that exquisite hair
That pleases ev'ry eye that longs for the beautiful and fair;
Her eyes were orbs of beauty, dark and crystal clear—
They never felt but once of pain and sorrow's bitter tear.

Her face was grandly formed, with cheeks of richest hue,
Which bore a gentle smile that told of a disposition true;
A pleasant and sweet nature in her could e'er be found—
She loved the ties of friendship, they 'rapt'd her bosom
    'round.

In them were found that noble heart that loved the rich and
    poor—
The latter always found a home within their open'd door—
The flowers that bloom'd beside those walls were never
    half so fair
As the fragrant buds that bloom'd within so tenderly and
    rare.

Their father, ere the last sweet bud had e'en begun to bloom,
Was borne away to a grassy hill to moulder in the tomb;
Beside that mound an angel-form has since been laid to
    rest—
Their mother—oh, what grief must then have swell'd each
    loving breast.

Alone in this changing world, with not a single tie
To bind them here, save the friends they held extremely
    nigh—
No relatives to call their own, save a distant one
Who lived away beyond their shore, 'neath the Western sun.

Time! on whose relentless wings life's joys are often borne,
Soon bore all their wealth away, leaving them here to mourn;
Here they lived awhile, but life became so lone and drear,
They moved away, and rented out the home they loved so
    dear.

Oft Eula's hand was sought in love, but that, alas! in vain;
Tho' many worshipped at her shrine, her hand they could
    not gain,
For 'round her heart in other days a pleasant tie did form
For one whose love was ever thus: constant and warm.

By his honest heart she was beloved, this she knew full well,
But in her hardly suited heart no love for him did dwell;
To her he was but a faithful friend on whom she could rely;
'If I marry him,' she often said, "I may love him by-and-by."

They were wedded on a balmy eve in the gentle month of
   May,
And passed from a distant cottage door—she beautiful and
   gay—
Now Eula and Eunita are as sad as girls can be,
For they are living all alone in that cottage by the sea.

A DIFFERENT TIDE.

(Written in a very handsome young lady's album the night before her
marriage, at the hour of twelve.)

Soon upon life's fitful ocean
   You shall meet a different tide,
And your loving bark be drifting
   To perhaps a brighter side.

Soon the past will be forgotten,
   Its hours absorbed in present bliss;
But can your loving heart forget
   The rapture of this parting kiss.

Some day within your memory
   Some sweet thought of me may glide,
Of pleasant hours spent together
   Ere you became another's bride.

TO MARIAN.

Thou art to me like the memory of a green hill
   Far away, where violets bloom here and there—
I love that hill, 'tis there I used to roam
   Ere I had felt or even dreamed of care.

MY OWN WORLD.

My life's a world—within my immortal soul
  There's a boundless realm
        No other being can control;
  None can hear, think, or feel for me,
  Be what I have been—and shall be.

In that strange world I may have oft found rest,
  And at times enjoyed
        Seasons of joy and happiness;
  But if any, alas! they have been few,
  And transient as the drops of morning dew.

And I have been the slave of those creations
  More difficult to subdue
        Than all earth's most hostile nations:—
  Passion, pride, lust—these Nature has secured
  In this weak bosom, and must ever be endured.

I'm on the throne of Time and Eternity,
  My strange courtiers are
        Sorrow, hope, ambition—all unfit
  To minister unto the sovereign will of one
  Whose life-star is as unchangeable as the sun.

Around that throne, in darkness and in light,
  I can always behold
        The being whom I once loved, still bright
  And sparkling in the zenith of her pride,
  Loving and being loved—a gentle bride.

Though in the tomb, neglected I shall lie,
  And even forgotten
        By those who once esteemed me high,
Yet that world of influence naught can dissever,
It must weary all ages and live on forever.

———

THOU OLD HYPOCRITE.

Oh, thou old gray-haired deceiver,
  Thou expounder of sacred Writ,
Dost thou not know that God in Heaven
  Dispises the hypocrite?

Thou art dead to ev'ry honest thought,
  And soon shall thy days expire;
Hell will be thy portion, thy reward—
  So prepare to meet its fire.

———

WOMAN'S LOVE.

How strangely warm is woman's love,
'Tis like summer to the wounded dove;
In pain and sorrow 'tis just the same
As on the dewy morn on which it came.

Yes, woman's love, indeed, is sweet,
Grows stronger when cast 'neath cruel feet;
'Twill live when other love is gone,
And comfort on the saddest morn.

TO MY MOTHER.

Mother, is it not in thy sweet name I live,
    And gather within me the richest joys of life?
Would not hope, love, ambition, all be nothing
    Without thee, and my days be but days of strife?

Have I not from the careless years of infancy
    Till now, honor'd and adored thy precious name?
Would not this weak and weary heart of mine
    Endure all things to shelter thee from blame?

Have I not 'mid the changing scenes of life
    Been always near thee to love thee more and more?
Have not these hands and feet grown truly strong
    In labor for thee—thou one whom I adore?

ONE WHO WOULD LINGER.

'Tis pleasant to be in a crowd of girls,
    And feel there's one you love the best;
One who is fair and sweet and kind,
    More beautiful than all the rest.

To know that her confidence and love
    Are center'd in your wayward heart;
To feel that you have one who'd linger
    Should all the other girls depart.

Oh, jealous heart that seeks to belittle my gentle muse,
    And blow your damnable bugle in my lonely ears;
You'll lie some day in expressing your recognition
    Of this very song you disowned in other years.

PERHAPS.

The moon-lit night was drear and lone,
  I heard a noise on yonder hill;
A human form came rushing by,
  Then all was calm and deathly still.

I recognized the slender form
  Passing from the cedar trees,
Clad in white, with raven hair
  Floating in the zephyr breeze.

Her white hands held the tissue folds,
  Thro' whose lace the moonbeams play'd
Upon her bosom—once so fair—
  Where no wayward hands had stray'd.

Perhaps the pearly gate of love
  And character was thrown ajar
To a sinful man—whose deeds the like,
  His character doth seldom mar.

The white rose decked her raven hair,
  But it had lost its beauty there;
A smile adorned her face, but not
  Like that which made her once so fair.

A glance revealed to her the fact
  That she was passing very nigh
To one who had esteemed her pure,
  For reasons I can ne'er deny.

May be she'd spied some erring man
  Who was seeking straw to make his bed;
Or had heard the hoot of the midnight-owl
  In the lonely tree limbs o'er her head.

MORE COSTLY THAN A DIAMOND RING.

Oh, character! thou ever art
  An holy and an honor'd thing;
More valuable than life itself,
  More costly than a diamond ring.

On thy fair finger, lovely maid,
  Let there no jewel ever be
If character be put at stake
  For the gem he has given thee.

Praised it may be by ev'ry one
  Whose eyes may look upon its glow;
But if by happiness it be bought,
  Each spark will be a spark of woe.

Many a glance may linger there,
  In admiration of the gift;
But, ah, no heart will sympathize
  Or from thy soul the burden lift.

As oft as thou wouldst gaze upon it
  This painful lesson thou must learn:
Earth's brightest jewel has its woe
  If PEACE be given in return.

———

SOLITUDE.

The sweetest, dearest spot on earth,
Where Truth alone is found,
  And no wayward feet intrude,
Is in that blessed shadow
Where we learn what we have been,
  And shall be—sweet Solitude.

MEMORIAL DAY IN COLUMBIA.

(On seeing a number of little girls clad in white march to the graves
of the Confederate dead and strew flowers thereon.)

'Round this hallow'd spot where lie
  The brave, the true, the honor'd dead,
Let youthful hands sweet garlands wreathe,
  And strew them o'er each silent head.

Oh, tender hearts, too young to feel
  The care which bore a soldier's sigh;
Gather the roses and strew them o'er
  These graves where truth and honor lie.

———

MAN'S LIFE.

Man's life is but a slender chain
Whose cold and rusty links
  Contain the deepest mystery;
Each particle may have its worth,
But ne'er will it be known to earth
  In the pages of history.

All save the good he may have done
In those changing hours
  Since childhood passed away,
Lie buried in the mould'ring folds
Of Oblivion's cold shroud—
  A monument of clay.

———

O that the lilies and roses were mine
Instead of the oak and ivy of life.

HOW STRANGE ARE DREAMS!

How strange are dreams!—I dreamed the other night
  A dream that made me tremble,
    Not with fear, but a kind of strange reality;
My supper, though late, consisted of no cheese,
  No salmonds, pies or wine had passed these lips.

How strange are dreams!—they carry us far away
  To scenes too long forgotten,
    Away back in our early childhood days,
Picturing our lives in a pure and simple way,
  Not as they were spent, nor when; but where.

How strange are dreams!—they have their boundless world,
  With trees, hills and lakes,
    And flowers of various kinds and hues—
Spirits of friends and loved ones long departed
  And perhaps too long forgotten—they are there.

How strange are dreams!—If death be like a dream—
  A pure and happy dream—
    How blissful and sweet must be our final end,
To emerge from a sinful world to find ourselves
  In dreams—dreaming through all eternity.

DISSIPATION.

Of all the sickening feelings
That swell the human breast,
  And worry the imagination,
None are so painful to the heart
As those at early morn
  After a night of dissipation.

Predicts Prohibition!

CARRIER'S ADDRESS.

(Written for THE STATE, Columbia, S. C., December 24th. 1893.)

"A merry Christmas, one and all!"
Heed the carrier's earnest call—
For a service long what will you do?—
He simply asks a "gift" of you.

By daylight damp, and e'en before,
He has thrown the news before your door,
And rarely has he e'er been late
With that welcom'd sheet, "The State."

"The State," that bears the honor'd seal
Of truth and justice, firm as steel;
Whose sentiments of truth will stand
Till justice permeates our land.

And while to-day in joy and mirth,
You gather 'round the family hearth,
Give cheerfully, and let it be
For a service render'd faithfully.

———

LITTLE ETHEL W——.

Sweet Ethel's years are only six—
    She's just six summers old;
But mine are twenty-six and one
    Long summers, damp and cold.

I love the smiles on Ethel's face,
    Alas! they are not few—
To me her azure eyes are like
    Sweet violets filled with dew.

(THIRD VOLUME.)

———

DEDICATED TO MY PATRONS THROUGHOUT
THE NORTH, EAST, AND WEST.

THE AUTHOR.

THE DEATH OF CHARLES A. DANA.

In all the firmament of the journalistic heavens,
'Mid the many twinkling stars of less resplendent light
   That scatter their silvery beams adown its mystic line,
The grandest literary orb that ever shed its rays
O'er the green-clad hills of this beloved land
   Has withdrawn its face from earth—never again to shine.

Never again to shine in all its full-orbed glory,
Bearing peace and justice alike to the rich and poor,
   Bright'ning the darkest caverns of the human mind—
Yet that resplendent glow has left a radiant light
That will grow and brighten as the years roll by,
   And leave a lasting impress on the hearts of mankind.

———

MY COUNTRY.

My Country! I love the stars upon thy glorious banner,
   Long may they shine o'er this my native land,
And tell to the millions yet unborn to earth
   Of thy glorious freedom won by valor's hand.

———

WOMAN.

Oh, that inexhaustible subject!
   Filled with celestial fire,
On which no seraph's song can cease,
   No poet's pen expire.
Oh, woman, delightful woman!
   In vain we long to be
Filled with that ennobling love,
   Found alone in thee.

BYRON.

Oh, thou immortal bard!
Men may condemn the song
    That issued from thy heart sublime,
Yet alas! its music sweet
Has left an echo that will sound
    Thro' the lone corridors of Time.

Thou immortal Byron!
Thy inspired genius
    Let no man attempt to smother—
May all that was good within thee
Be attributed to Heaven,
    All that was evil—to thy mother.

MY LOVELY VENUS.

Oh, thou, my lovely Venus!
If I were a star in the heavens,
    And should on thy countenance shine,
I would hide my glowing face,
And fall into nothingness
    At the foot of thy sacred shrine.

MY COUNTRY.

My Country! I love thy dewy hills and dales,
    And the buttercups and violets in thy meadows fair,
I love the balmy breeze from off thy pleasant wood,
    And the sweet notes of birds that swell thy peaceful air.

CLOSE BY HER BOSOM.

Close by her bosom let me sleep
After I've laid this body down,
          Adown to die;
And in stillness sweet, forever
Beside her pure, angelic form,
          There let me lie.

Her raven hair may some day grow,
And like the tender ivy, find
          Some open place
Beneath the lid of her lone pall,
And gath'ring in my grave may cling
          Around my face.

Plant o'er my head the fragrant rose
That oft adorned her silken hair,
          That it may wave
And shed its sweet perfume above
Her sacred face, beloved, adored,
          Within the grave.

I'll not hear her gentle voice,
Nor view her smiling face again,
          While sleeping there;
But at the first dawn of the morn
When we arise, I'll kiss her face,
          And kiss her hair.

His loving voice will bid us come
And join the snow-white throng upon
          That golden strand;

We'll pass within the pearly gates
And thro' the New Jerusalem,
　　With hand in hand.

———

TWO LOVED ONES IN HEAVEN.

(On the death of two lovely girls who passed away a short time since
in this city.)

How dark are the shadows that linger to-night
'Round the home that was once so lovely and bright —
Death's angel has passed o'er the family hearth,
And plucked from its circle the fairest of earth.

A broken-hearted mother sits weeping to-night
O'er two loved ones far away from her sight ;
But she sees 'mid her darkness the beautiful light
Of that Saviour who guided their footsteps aright.

Sweet Annie and Mary were the treasures of life,
Whose hearts knew nothing of anger and strife—
So lovely they were in the morning of youth
Their faces were beaming with beauty and truth.

Their days were too few to be ended so soon
By death's cold hand ere the fullness of noon,
And e'en tho' fever was burning their cheek
Of their heavenly home they did frequently speak.

It was harder than all to whisper farewell
To these dear ones we have always loved so well ;
To see them depart in their innocent bloom
In the morning of life, adown to the tomb.

But deep in our bosoms their memory'll be borne,
And their faces be to us like the spring-tide morn—
Their names will be cherish'd for that sweet love
They revealed to man and their Saviour above.

On some sweet day when this weary life is o'er
We'll greet their happy smiles on the other shore—
And from Annie and Mary who have gone before
We ne'er again can part—no, never more.

A BROKEN TIE.

Oh, Time! thou changer and justifier of all things,
  Tell me, thou raven or white-wing'd dove;
Tell me, while on thy winged wings I soar,
  Shall I e'er see again the object of my love?

Have I not loved ONE beautiful and fair,
  Who in other days lay nearest to my breast?
Tell me, while on thy fleeting wings I sigh,
  Shall her head e'er again on my bosom rest?

Oh, Time! have I not suffer'd all for her?—
  In memory have I not grief and pain withstood?—
Hope, love, ambition, have they not all been lost,
  Buried in her being—the goddess of the good?

Have I not seen in youth my fondest hope
  Grow dim and steal away, I know not where?
Grief, pain, regret, have they not turned
  This heart, these eyes, to one embitter'd tear?

Tell me!—in thy strange, relentless flight,
  Canst thou not stop to mend a broken tie?—
That tie is Love and fond Affection
  For HER, the beautiful, for whom I sigh.

JUST SIMPLY GRAND.

In lovely attitude she stood,
  With beaming face, in a happy mood—
      I wished her mine;
Like a crimson rose in the dewy morn
  Her face was fair to look upon—
      So rich, divine.

I couldn't but love her snowy neck,
In beauty grand, without a speck,
      Or trace at all;
And looking then at her pretty feet,
I praised that lower gift complete
      And very small.

Like the leaves of the summer rose
Were her pink cheeks and pretty nose,
      Just simply grand;
And looking on her milk-white arms,
I felt inspired by their charms,
      And press'd her hand.

Traveler, view yon lovely mansion
  Won at the cost of a widow's tears—
Naught but a vacant lot you'll see
  When you come this way in other years.

FOOTPRINTS BY THE MILL.

Green is the moss that clusters around
  The door of this lonely old mill;
I can see my gentle Mary's foot prints
  Deep traced in the green moss still.

The old rail fence o'er which she climb'd
  On many a balmy summer day,
Like the dark mill house is cover'd with moss,
  Broken down and mould'ring away.

Ne'er would I speak of this gloomy old spot
  That contains not a scene that is fair,
If my Mary's feet had not linger'd 'round,
  And left their sweet imprints there.

My Mary was a lovely, dark-eyed girl,
  With soft brown hair and smiling face,
And slender form of that perfect mold
  That shows a world of truth and grace.

Sad is the mem'ry of this dreary old mill,
  And the green moss 'round its lonely door;
For Mary whom I loved in other years
  Has passed away to return no more.

She passed while the golden sun was sinking
  On a cloudless eve in the month of May;
She gave up the life that might have been mine
  Had she not passed so early away.

While these lone and dreary scenes I view,
  And I list to the sighing winds above,
I can almost see my Mary's face,
  And hear her tender words of love.

Order Form--JGC

Prof. C. H. Neuffer
  USC English Dept
  Columbia, S.C. 29208

Inclosed check for $_____. Send ___
copies of PURELY ORIGINAL VERSE by
J. Gordon Coogler (Neuffer-LaBorde
reprint, 1974), each copy $6.00, to:

        Name _____

        Address _____

        City _____

        State _____   ZIP _____

We'd appreciate your sending us names
and addresses of other persons who'd
like to know of this Coogler reprint,
available only by mail-order.

FOOTPRINTS BY THE MILL.

Green is the moss that clusters around
   The door of this lonely old mill;
I can see my gentle Mary's footprints
   Deep traced in the green moss still.

Her life was dear to me in early youth,
   And dearer still it grew in after years;
To-day in memory of that life of love,
   I'll bathe her footprints with my warmest tears.

She was poor, but that she could not help,
   It was her lot and she was not to blame,
Yet she retained 'mid all her poverty
   That grandest thing in life—a spotless name.

I loved her because she was poor and kind,
   And bore a heart that often beat too true;
She was constant, and when my love grew weak
   She ne'er once dreamed of turning unto you.

She was too fair a rose to bloom alone,
   Encircled by the dangerous thorns of earth—
She died, but will bloom again in Heaven
   The same sweet rose—but of nobler birth.

FAREWELL TO THOSE MOMENTS.

We used to stroll ofttimes together
In spring-tide's cool and balmy weather,
   O'er many a hill and meadow green;
But now she strolls in a distant land,
Her feet upon the sinking sand,
   Heart broken and less serene.

I used to hold her pretty hand
Long ere it wore another's band,
   And kiss it o'er and o'er again;
But now those moments loved so well
Do but in my memory dwell
   To bear a joy mixed with pain.

HILLS, ROADS, A VALLEY AND A FOUNTAIN.

(It was the author's pleasure not many years since, while in the "Land of Flowers," to become thoroughly acquainted with the picturesque scenery as described in the following poem.)

There was a time when the fire of youth
　　Burn'd deep within my wayward soul,
I often stroll'd o'er pleasant hills,
　　Where timid mortals seldom stroll.

Those hills were never cover'd o'er
　　With nature's cold and chilly dew;
But damp with heaven's melting drops,
　　They were ever charming to my view.

Mine eyes had never seen before
　　Such lovely hills as met their gaze;
My soul was in a paradise
　　Where it alone could sweetly graze.

'Round that lone spot no cypress tree
　　E'er waved with leaves of gold or green;
But flowers as pure as the lily's leaf
　　Lent beauty to the charming scene.

A zephyr sweet from off those hills
　　Was wafted from a fount below,
Where tender sprigs of golden grass
　　Glisten'd in the moonbeam's glow.

The vale between those dewy hills
　　Was ne'er so enticing to mine eyes
As when the moonbeam's silvery rays
　　Played on it from the midnight skies.

Serene and quiet were those hills
   Where oft my famish'd soul had fed;
But more serene was the lovely vale
   Where at times I laid my weary head.

Oft have I lain at twilight eve
, With buoyant heart and tired feet
Beside the wild, romantic flowers,
   That cluster'd 'round that fountain sweet.

Two balmy roads led to the fount,
   Where never wayward feet had been
Save mine—for it was chiefly mine
   To roam and meditate therein.

Oft have I ruffled the golden grass
   That waved in beauty day and night
Beside that fount—but in my haste
   On a summer eve I took my flight.

Those hills to me are pleasant still,
   And will be till I'm old and gray;
That dewy vale with its loved incline
   Is where my head is wont to lay.

That fount is still a lovely spot,
   If the grass retains its golden hue—
The balmy roads are pleasant yet,
   If sprinkled with the fountain's dew.

———

As the ivy twines the lily's leaf 'neath the forest tree,
So 'mid the changing scenes of life I cling to thee.

THE AUTUMN LEAVES.

I hear the lonely autumn breeze
Sighing thro' the half-clad maple trees
     'Round yonder cot;
The golden leaves how swiftly they fly
While the dreary branches seem to sigh,
     Is this OUR lot?

I see them falling unto the earth
That gave their stately parents birth,
     Like flakes of gold;
I see them resting on the meadow grass,
Lying 'round me in a golden mass—
     In earth to mould.

How strange that gentle spring should bear
Its tender leaves for autumn's air
     To fade away,
And fall in death!—that cruel thing
That has, alas! a venomed sting
     For mortal clay.

WORLDLY PLEASURE.

E'en tho' by pursuit we honestly gain it,
  No satisfaction that knowledge would bring;
For soon we'd grow tired and hate to begin it,
  And cast it aside—a detestable thing.

The joy in pleasure is when we pursue it,
  The HOPE, not the object pursuit would attain;
For the object is transient—hope is eternal;
  Pursuit has its joy—to gain has its pain.

FALSE, UNGRATEFUL, UNKIND.

Far from thy presence would to God I could flee,
For I'm weary of the pain I have gather'd from thee;
That pain too fresh and too deep in my heart
For the soul of forgiveness ever to part.

Thou art even as false as some frivolous youth
Who has rejected all honor and discarded the truth ;
Thy hand at this moment is colder than death,
And the words from thy lips are but poisonous breath.

Thou art fair to behold, but thy bosom is hard,
And contains not a feeling I now can regard ;
For thou hast been false, ungrateful, unkind—
The good that lay in thee I never could find.

————

IN THE WILDS OF MY SOUL.

I love to roam in the wilds of my soul
  Where birds sing sweetly and flowers are fair;
Where there are streamlets, lakes and ponds,
  With naught to beset or tempt me there.

I love to sit by that rippling stream
  Whose waters no eyes can e'er behold
Save these longing eyes of mine,
  In that sweet world to mortals untold.

I love to list to the birds in the trees
  As they warble their notes on the stilly air ;
And I love to be with the beautiful flowers
  That bloom in the wilds of my soul so fair.

TWILIGHT ON THE FARM.

'Tis pleasant to see the broom-sedge burning
  At evening twilight on the farm ;
To see the weary cows returning,
  And hear the peacock's wild alarm.

'Tis pleasant to see the rabbit playing
  In the sand beside the lonely mill;
To hear the watch-dog faintly baying
  Some object o'er the distant hill.

'Tis pleasant to see the dove returning
  To its long deserted, gloomy nest ;
To hear the little sparrow yearning
  For its limb of quietude and rest.

'Tis pleasant to hear the gentle maiden
  Singing 'mid the garden's bowers;
To see her peaceful bosom laden
  With its fairest budding flowers.

———

P——D and B——E.

It must have been LOVE that could stoop to the plain
Of shame and disgrace and endure such pain
For one whose passion o'erbalanced his honor,
As shown by the suffering he imposed upon her.

It must have been LOVE that could drink from the spring
Of the gall of bitterness—knowing 'twould bring
Eternal disgrace—the purity of life
Forfeited for the hope of becoming a wife.

REPOSING.

(On being asked by a pretty brown-eyed girl, in the month of August, to write a poem for her while she reposed. The following lines were presented to her on her awakening.)

As I stand beside thy lovely form,
    And see those gentle eyelids close,
I feel I'm standing by an angel
    Falling into sweet repose.

As I view thy snowy neck 'and face,
    I wish that they were only mine ;
My heart grows weary for repose
    Beside that tender heart of thine.

I love those eyes e'en when closed,
    And too I love that pretty nose—
Thy velvet cheeks they are to me
    Like the leaves of the summer rose.

I love that sweet, half-open'd mouth,
    With ivory teeth as white as pearl—
Ah, yes, to me 'tis untold bliss
    To stand beside this sleeping girl.

A MISTAKE.

(The poem containing three verses, published in my second book and entitled "That Christmas Card," are the only verses in my life which I regret ever having written. The entire poem is a mistake caused by being too hasty.)

I would willingly forfeit my right to the muse
    If I only this day could recall
The verses I wrote in the heat of my passion,
    Which I consider the meanest of all.

POOR FELLOW, HE'S DEAD.

Kind friends, you like me while I'm gay,
    And the jolly tide of youth flows on;
But you will never think of me
    After I'm laid away and gone.

You'll never think of him who loved
    And breathed for you a gracious breath;
Ah, no, you'll e'er forget the hands
    You gently cross'd in stilly death.

You'll forget all the friendly smiles
    That I ever for you have shed,
And if my name should e'er be called,
    You'd say, "Poor fellow, he's dead!"

ANNIE, THE MOCKING-BIRD.

O would I were a mocking-bird
    Like the one that sings for me,
I'd keep my lovely throat in tune,
    And warble in ev'ry tree.

I'd sing to lonely human hearts,
    And cheer them day by day;
At night I'd charm the poet's ear
    With my very sweetest lay.

Long would I sit beside his door
    And warble his "Marguerite,"
And too I'd sing "The Mocking-Bird"
    In accents gay and sweet.

THERE'S BLISS FOR YOU.

'Mid life's many changing scenes,
 Clouds may gather o'er your way;
Yet behind their gloomy shadows
 There's for you a brighter day.

Disappointment fast may come,
 As hope upon its wings expires;
But faith and love will bring to pass
 Your fondest wishes and desires.

IN MEMORIAL.

(To a young lady who sought publicity by attempting to belittle in
public print a poem by the author, entitled "Beautiful Snow"—She has
never been heard from through the press since.)

She died after the beautiful snow had melted,
 And was buried beneath the "slush;"
The last sad words she breathed upon earth
 Were these simple ones, "Oh, poet, do hush!"

famous lyric

CHILDHOOD SCENES.

O raptured scenes of childhood hours !
 In memory I behold
Thy dewy paths and grassy hills
 Where oft my feet have stroll'd.

ALONE.

I feel like some lone, deserted lad,
Standing on the shore of life's great ocean
Casting pebbles in its billows, as if to excite
 Some past emotion.

THE MEMORY OF THY FACE.

My mem'ry calls me back when I first saw thy face,
  Those moments in my life that are dearest of all—
To the hour when I met thee in beauty and grace,
  That hour of rapture I delight to recall.

As I stand by thy shrine of beauty and truth
  I paint me a picture no artist can paint—
A picture of thee in the bloom of thy youth,
  Fair as the lily and as pure as a saint.

The love that exists in that bosom of thine
  Is as perfect as the bloom on thy beautiful face,
Thus fain I would kneel at the foot of thy shrine
  And there be absorb'd in thy beauty and grace.

I speak not to flatter thee, remember this well,
  As the mem'ry of thy face this day I recall—
For deep in my bosom thy spirit doth dwell,
  And thou to that bosom art dearer than all.

Thy smiles are as soft as the sunbeam's ray
  When it kisses the hills in the distant west;
They light up my soul from day unto day,
  And bring to my life eternal, sweet rest.

Thou art a charm to my wandering eye,
  The flower of my hope—a milk-white dove;
And a star in the east in the cloudless sky,
  More beautiful to me than an angel of love.

———

This life is but a fleeting scene of trials and sorrow,
A faint ray of hope to-day, a dismal cloud to-morrow.

THERE'LL BE MY TOMB.

I'm in the world, a world of sighs,
Of sorrow, pain and weeping eyes,
    And ofttimes gloom ;
I love the few sweet sunny hours
I've spent amid the woodland flowers—
    There'll be my tomb.

My tomb! but ah, I'm loath to die,
And 'neath those lovely flowers lie
    Mould'ring away;
They'll bloom sweetly, but in that tomb
I'll not scent their sweet perfume,
    Each silent day.

Sweet summer with its peaceful calm
Will bear a pure and holy balm
    Around that mound ;
But alas ! no boon 'twill bring to me,
For I'll not feel, or hear or see,
    Beneath the ground.

Then what care I to leave a name
Praised for genius, wealth or fame,
    When I am gone;
Such praises as your lips would bear
I'd not care to hear up there,
    Beside God's throne.

———

There's many an angel in the hovels of earth,
 'Mid the lonely shades of the forest pine,
Hidden from the view of the passer-by
 By the gloomy leaves of the ivy vine.

OUR FINAL HOME.

Just above us—not a score of miles away,
We'll spend our vast eternity—some day;
A blessed abode where all is pure and fair—
Spirits of many loved ones gone—they are there.

The JUST alone—those who have loved on earth,
And much sorrow endured—of lowly birth;
They shall wing their way thro' realms sublime,
Naught shall mar their flight—not even Time.

Floating mansions will be there, and walls of gold,
And gates of pearls, these shall our eyes behold;
And streets whose surface purest gold shall grace,
Will be our grand, eternal home—in SPACE.

Naught but the gentle, the sinless and the fair,
Can inhale the fragrance of that heavenly air,
Where flowers bloom in love, and the sunlight is clear,
And no eyelids are heavy with sorrow and care.

Death is like a dream—a pure and simple dream;
A peaceful voyage upon a peaceful stream;
A stream whose waters—unlike the troubled sea—
Will bear our frail bark on to Eternity.

"FAREWELL!"

This word to a youthful heart is solemn,
    And one on which I would not dwell;
But to-night it must be spoken,
    So unto you I say—"farewell!"

TO MY MOTHER.

Lean on this bosom, 'tis for thee it doth swell,
It shall bear thee, support thee, and comfort thee well;
Not a thought, not a word in life I would speak
That would bear for a moment a tear to thy cheek.

Lean on this bosom, 'tis for thee it doth swell,
No other is so worthy in its chamber to dwell;
An angel of peace thou art unto me—
I forget all my sorrows while thinking of thee.

Lean on this bosom, for 'tis given to thee;
A touch of thy being bears strength unto me;
The smile on thy face, like the smile of the morn,
Will live in my heart when all others are gone.

———

A MUSTACHELESS BARD.

His whiskers didn't come, his mustache is gone,
  And to-day he's standing ashore
Enjoying the breeze with a cleaned shaved lip,
  Relieved of the burden it bore.

He's feeling so lonely, dull and forsaken,
  The boys they know him no more;
The girls are surprised, and speaking of him,
  Say, "He's uglier than ever before."

He can't understand why the beautiful girls
  Should thus be so cruel and rash,
Unless they believe that kisses are sweeter
  From lips that bear a mustache.

MAY ALL THESE BE THINE, MAYME.

May thy cheeks be as soft and sweet
As the hyacinths 'round thy gentle feet,
And may those lovely eyes of thine
Like stars of beauty ever shine.

May thy soft locks of raven hair
Lend beauty to thy neck so fair,
And may thy bosom, pure and white,
Be ever filled with Truth and Right.

May thy sweet life be naught but love,
And gentle like the turtle dove;
And may thy hand be free to do
All that's noble, kind and true.

———

There's something sweetly solemn
In the moonbeam's silvery rays,
Bearing thoughts of other years,
Their melancholy days.

———

There's nothing in life to live for,
Except it be sorrow and pain;
But there's more in death than dying
To simply exist again. .

———

Turn the light of Truth into the chamber of your soul,
And there let it glow like a radiant star;
It will dispel all the sickening shadows therein,
And show you, poor mortal, just what you are.

'TIS HARD TO BE HAPPY.

I wish I was happy, but that cannot be
While I'm drifting on life's changeable sea;
Ever toss'd by the waves is my frail little bark,
As on to Eternity it floats in the dark.

I wish I was happy, but that cannot be
While the grave with its terrors lies open for me,
As I look into its bosom so lonely and cold
My soul is absorbed in mystery untold.

In mystery untold!—for no mortal knows
The gloom and the shadow of that chilly repose—
O'ershadow'd as I am, and if that shadow be true,
'Tis enough for this soul without punishment too.

To that monster Death I'm but a weak slave,
Drawn down by his hand to the horrible grave,
And I cannot escape, but must suffer my doom,
To lay down forever in darkness and gloom.

'Tis hard to be happy since hope has been lost
In the changes of life, with its sunshine and frost,
While the grave's cold bosom lies open for me,
As my frail bark floats on to Eternity.

———

TO THE POOR YOUNG MAN.

'Tis better to part from the girl you love
  The one whom you adore,
If that dark eyed sister in your home
  Loves to slam the door.

AN EMPTY VASE.

(On seeing an empty vase, covered with dust, in a room once bright
with the smiles of a lovely Christian girl; but now deserted, and bearing
the odor of faded flowers.)

Tho' it sits upon the mantle
   In a lone and dusty place,
Yet it bears the pleasant mem'ry
   Of a kind and happy face.

The face of one departed
   From the shades of earthly gloom,
Whose tender smiles still linger,
   Tho' she sleeps in the silent tomb.

That hand so kind and lovely
   Moves no longer there
To deck that vase and mantle
   With flowers rich and fair.

Who knew her tender thoughts
   As she plucked the lilac bloom
And bore it to this lonely vase,
   Still sitting in the room.

But that vase is empty now,
   Those hands are cold and gone;
The lilac buds therein no more
   Will bloom on summer's morn.

————

I had rather hear an earthquake
   As it roars 'neath hill and valley,
Than to hear those angry under-tones
   From the pouting lips of Salley.

BEWARE OF YOUR CHARACTER.

Beware of your character, my charming young girl,
Keep it near to your heart as a priceless pearl ;
There are thieves who would steal from your hand and arm,
And then rob your bosom of its costliest charm.

Beware of your character, my charming young girl,
Deceit has a dagger which at you it would hurl,
And men of the world would smile if the dart
Was destroying the peace of your innocent heart.

Beware of your character, my charming young girl,
As a banner of purity may it ever unfurl,
And the hearts of all men be led to admire
That character aglow with a heavenly fire.

CIRCUMSTANCES.

In Circumstances chilly hand,
O'er a dangerous gulf we stand,
 Hungry and sore ;
No human hand can save us there,
We must endure our own despair
 Forever more.

Oh, Circumstances! what e'er thou art,
Thy hands have sever'd many a heart
 Naught else could sever;
Tho' Time should part thy cruel grasp,
Yet the impress of its clasp,
 Will bleed forever.

MEMORY'S PICTURE.

In my memory there's a picture I love to behold
Of a face whose meaning has never been told ;
'Tis lovelier than the white-robed clouds in the west
As they downward move to where the sunbeams rest.

That picture is painted in colors not as bold
As earth's flashy hues of purple and gold—
The artist that painted it came from above,
With TRUTH his brush, and his colors were LOVE.

As I look in those eyes that are dearest to me
In those charming blue orbs heaven I see ;
My thoughts are borne away to the skies
As I gaze with rapture in those sweet eyes.

As I picture that face so blissful, divine,
There's a feeling of joy in this bosom of mine ;
But 'tis mingled with grief that I should behold
That face whose meaning I cannot unfold.

As I view with pleasure that dove-like form
I see the embodiment of friendship warm ;
And my soul with its love would nevermore sigh
If that form—not its picture—was ling'ring nigh.

————

A MONUMENT OF LOVE.

My love shall remain thro' endless time
A monument to thy love sublime
    I now adore ;
No marble pillar shall mark the spot—
Let the violet and forget-me-not
    Bloom evermore.

NOT SATISFIED.

Though we go in the field where the lilies are blooming
        In all their gentle pride,
Yet we'll feel like a stranger, and a pilgrim forever,
    For after all
        We are not satisfied.

Though we sit 'mid the shade of the far-reaching oak,
        And by the daisies abide,
We'll still feel forsaken and alone in the world,
    For after all,
        We are not satisfied.

Though we lay near the brook on the cool, green moss,
        And turn from side to side,
We'll still feel neglected and sadly undone,
    For after all
        We are not satisfied.

Though we watch the flow of the beautiful river,
        As its waters subside,
We'll still feel unhappy and ever so weary,
    For after all
        We are not satisfied.

Though we sit near the angel that shines by the hearth;
        She in our love confide,
We'll still be in sorrow and acquainted with grief,
    Longing for rest
        And never satisfied.

Though we stand by the fountain that's flowing with love
        And drink of its sweet tide,
We'll still bear the feeling and doleful assurance:
    Love is bitter—
        We are not satisfied.

REMEMBER'D SMILES.

(On the death of Miss E. W., a charming young lady, and a devoted
Christian, who passed away some time since in this city.)

Beautiful smiles, remember'd smiles,
   They come like sunbeams from the cloudless west;
They come from the face and the peaceful heart
   Of a loved one now in her home of rest.

They speak of a lovely, purified soul,
   Whose life was as pure as the air she breathed ;
They tell of the beauty of the home she loved,
   Of the Christ she sought, and never deceived.

They tell of the rapture, beautiful rapture,
   Of a life well spent in this vale of tears,
They show as the dew drops show the flower,
   That Heaven has a balm for mortal cares.

They tell of a lowly, crucified One
   Whose smiles were to her like a sunbeam's kiss;
They speak as she spoke in a world of sin :
   "Jesus, to love Thee is rapturous bliss."

———

LYDIE'S SWEET DARK EYES.

Her dark eyes—I love to gaze within them
   Whene'er I pass that shady spot
      'Round that loved door;
Fain would I pause when she is there,
And gazing on her face and hair,
      Would love her more.

(SECOND VOLUME.)

TREAD SOFTLY.

Tread softly, oh, you mortal man
　　As you journey here below,'
There's many a pure and lovely rose
　Where'er your footsteps go.

There's many a rose bud drooping low
　　That once was fresh and sweet,
Now perishing for want of care
　　Beneath your wayward feet.

Oft 'mid the dingy autumn leaves
　　The rose sheds a brighter hue,
But only thro' the grace of God,
　　And his sweet morning dew.

There's many a sweet and lonely bud
　　That's bending in the clay,
While you go heedlessly along
　　Life's bright and happy way.

Tread softly, oh, you mortal man,
　　Don't cease to watch and fear
Lest you should pass some fallen one
　　Who needs your love and care.

———

WRITTEN FOR AN ALBUM.

Time may stain this spotless page,
　　And these simple lines erase ;
But it cannot dim the mem'ry
　　Of thy well-beloved face.

NO AUTUMN IN THE HEART.

The yellow leaves are falling, love,
   The summer will soon be o'er,
And we are no nearer to-day, love,
   Than we have been before.

The tender bloom of youth, love,
   Is fastly growing adim,
And soon 'twill fade away, love,
   As the leaves on yonder limb.

Our hands will soon grow cold, love,
   Our footsteps be in grief;
Our weary heads will droop, love,
   As droops the autumn leaf.

No autumn in the heart, love,
   Shall come to you and me,
Tho' we'll be lone at night, love,
   As the leafless autumn tree.

Deep grief will come to us, love,
   Which we can never part;
Tho' sore it cannot bring, love,
   Sad autumn in the heart.

———

A PRETTY GIRL.

On her beautiful face there are smiles of grace
   That linger in beauty serene,
And there are no pimples encircling her dimples
   As ever, as yet, I have seen.

SOME DAY.

Some day—it may be while the sun is sinking
  Slowly in the distant west,
I will cross that unknown river, mother,
  To that sunny shore of rest.

Some day, when the smile of loved ones gone
  Bids me come to yonder shore,
I'll meet and kiss you, and be with you,
  And see your face forevermore.

Some day, when life's dim star has flicker'd out,
  I'll bid adieu to earthly care—
I'll leave behind no false impression
  Of the life spent while with you here.

————

'TIS OF THEE THAT I THINK.

'Tis of thee that I think when the twilight is dawning,
  And the night shade of gloom is parted and gone,
And Nature with joy awakes from her slumber
  To welcome with pride the beautiful morn.

'Tis of thee that I think when the sun is advancing
  Its life-giving beams on all nature around;
Its smiles—like thine—to my soul are enchanting,
  And remind me of thee, where pleasures abound.

'Tis of thee that I think when the twilight of evening
  Is gathering around this bosom of mine,
Shedding a glimmer in the portals of hope
  Where my joy and peace lie buried in thine.

THAT RED HAT.

I love that broad-brim'd, stylish hat,
   All covered o'er with crimson red;
I love it because 'tis often seen
   Upon my darling's precious head.

I love the smiles beneath that brim
   On which my soul has often fed;
I love them, for they sweetly glow
   In beauty 'neath a crimson red.

I love those youthful, precious strands,
   Of silken, soft and downy hair;
I love them, for they cluster 'round
   My darling's neck so pure and fair.

I love those cheeks of velvet hue;
   Like flowers in a dewy bed;
I love that girl, and love that hat
   All cover'd o'er with crimson red.

"YOUNG MANHOOD."

In passion's wayward stream we float,
   A strange and irresistless tide;
Reckless thoughts, suggestive words,
   Oft greet our ears on either side.

"Young manhood" is not all in name,
   A dull, obscure, unmeaning term—
Nor is it like the lifeless tree
   That has forever lost its germ.

A GOLDEN HAIRED GIRL.

Fair lady I'll admit that I've loved in the past,
    And at many a shrine have knelt ;
But I knew not the depth of my hearts true love
    Till a glance from your eyes I had felt.

But that smile is not mine on your rose-tinted cheeks,
    Nor that sunlight of hope in your eyes;
Yet gladly I love them, for I know they are true,
    And as constant as the stars in the skies.

Your hair is a treasure, so silken and soft,
    Oft gather'd into one bright fold ;
It bears the rich hue that I always admired—
    A beautiful California gold.

There's a harp in your bosom that bears many notes,
    The sweetest these lonely ears have heard ;
Its strings are divine, for they tell me of love
    In soft notes that outrival the bird.

Adieu, fair lady! if no more we should meet,
    And your sweet form be drifted apart,
Yet the sacred mem'ry of your matchless face
    I will ever keep fresh in my heart.

————

BUT FEW VIRTUES.

The Colonels
Lady &
mistress

O'Grady

Many are the great men the world has produced
    Whose virtues, alas! have been few;
For they have drank in sin with as much delight
    As the butterfly drinks the dew.

A GRACIOUS FRIEND.

(Written by request on the fly-leaf of a young lady's Bible.)

Earthly friends may prove untrue
  And coldly on thee look,
But thou wilt have a lasting friend
  If trusting in this Book.

Dark clouds may gather o'er thy head,
  And hover 'round thee near;
But this Book will be a beacon light
  To guide thy feet from fear.

Cold hands may touch thy gentle hand
  Whom long thy love forsook ;
But thou wilt hold a gracious hand
  If trusting in this Book.

———

VOCAL MUSIC.

That sweetly sad melody
That comes from the golden strings
  Of that tender'st of harps—the heart.
So strange, so sweetly strange
It gives that to the human soul
  Which angels cannot impart.

That fond harp of a thousand
Ever-tuned, invisible strings,
  Swelled by the touch of sacred love ;
So strange, so sweetly strange,
It often bears, and it alone,
  The vilest heart to heaven above.

ALONE AT MIDNIGHT ON THE CONGAREE.

I watched the moon at the midnight hour
  As it slowly sunk to the distant west;
It looked like an angel clothed in white,
  Softly stealing to its home of rest.

I watched it pass 'hind the fleeting clouds,
  As it cast its shadows down upon me;
Then again it would scatter its silvery rays
  On the lonely hills by the Congaree.

I watched it until the distant clouds
  Gather'd in the west and passed away;
Then I beheld in its matchless beauty
  That mystic circle—the milkyway.

I thought of the millions of human souls
  That have watched its light on land and sea,
And of the thousands who in other days
  Have watched it by old Congaree.

I thought as it sunk in the far-off west,
  And withdrew from my view its last fond ray,
How sweet if my life like that silvery orb
  Could peacefully and quietly steal away.

DON'T WOUND HER FEELINGS.

Young man, don't wound her feelings
  With words that are cold and rough,
For life with its vicissitudes
  Will wound them soon enough.

Tempus fugit

PASSING AWAY.

Everything passes away in its turn,
Teaching the sad lesson we all must learn;
The breeze that cooled your cheek is gone,
Never to cool it again in the morn.

not bad!

The flowers that sweetly bloom in the lane
Will fade and never be seen there again;
The swamp's fair lily and green-clad fern,
Will pass from their bed and never return.

The birds that chirp about in the trees,
Are passing away like the morning breeze;
All pass to their destiny void of regard
For their Maker, Sustainer, Adorable God.

The dark river-water that flows in its course
Can never again return to its source;
And the crystal water that's deep in the well
Is bidding its source a lasting farewell.

And man! one immortal, with senses of right,
With heaven in his soul and God in his sight,
Must pass like the rest, each in his turn,
On to the grave, never to return.

———

I'LL ONLY THINK OF THEE.

Miss Annie, as oft in solitude
As whene'er 'tis mine to be,
I'll silence ev'ry wayward thought,
And only think of thee.

THINKING OF THEE.

In the quiet hours of the night,
As the cricket chirps upon the hearth,
　　　I'm prone to be
Sadly wandering, sadly lurking,
'Round some old familiar spot
　　　Alone with thee.

As I list to the ticking of the clock,
As it ticks away the midnight hour,
　　　Its solemn sound
Sadly echoes, sadly deepens,
As it bears my heart to thee
　　　Where peace is found.

As I list to the earliest pipe
Of the half-awaken'd mocking-bird
　　　In the elm tree,
There's a whisper, gentle whisper,
That tells my soul that some sweet day
　　　I'll be with thee.

———

SLEEP, SWEET CHILD.

(On a child's grave.)

Sleep, sweet child in thy little bed,
　Flowers are blooming o'er thy head—
The daisies fair and violets sweet
　Shall ever cluster 'round thy feet.

Sleep, sweet child, in thy little bed,
　No wind shall murmur o'er thy head;
But the gentle breeze of love shall wave
　Each dewy flower o'er thy grave.

TO LYDIE.

As the last rays of sunset are fading away,
    This eve I think of thee,
And picture thy sweet face in all its beauty,
    So fondly dear to me.

I think of thee while gazing on the western clouds
    Tinged with purest gold ;
And treasure thee as one far dearer to me
    Than all I now behold.

I think of thee while sitting on the cool, sweet grass,
    And looking o'er the park,
And wonder if this heart will e'er be lighted
    By thy ennobling spark.

———

THE CUP OF SORROW.

This weary life is filled with grief,
With sorrow deep, and we've no relief
From that overflowing cup
Which we must drink of, sup by sup.

'Tis sad that we live to droop and die,
With no kind friend to linger nigh,
And no sweet voice that gently speaks,
Or hand to touch our burning cheeks.

'Tis sad that we hold life's bitter cup,
Only to drink of it, sup by sup ;
To know we cannot lay it by,
But must drink, alas! and slowly die.

SHE'S VERY DEAR TO ME.

There's a little brown eyed lady
   Who is very dear to me,
She occupies a lovely cottage
   'Mid the oaks in Waverly.

She's a pretty, smiling lady,
   But I seldom see her smiles,
For our homes are far apart,
   Just about two dreary miles.

I'm very fond of this sweet lady,
   For she has such beaming eyes;
But if I procrastinate
   Another heart may win the prize.

She's a polished, noble lady,
   Highly learned, industrious too,
And her sunny hand is faithful
   In whate'er it finds to do.

In my being there's no object
   That can fill its better part
Save this little brown eyed lady—
   She is nearest to my heart.

TEARS.

Tears! they always tell a tale
   No human knowledge can avail
To solve, or find the meaning true
   Of those pure drops of sacred dew.

TO ELEANORE.

Fond as the remember'd kisses of lips now in the grave
  Is that sweet face of thine ;
Of kisses when the heart reposed in sweeter hope
  Than this vain hope of mine.

Dear as the remember'd smiles on youth's unsullied cheek
  In boyhood's dewy morn,
Are thy sweet and tender smiles to me so fondly dear,
  In beauty ever borne.

Fond as the summer's morn when the maiden's sweet hand
  Gathers the lilac bloom,
Are those endearing smiles upon thy lovely face,
  Dispelling my inmost gloom.

Loved as the remember'd notes of music on the air
  From a voice most divine,
Are those enchanting notes that swell my lonely heart
  With that sweet love of thine.

PULL OF THOSE SUSPENDERS.

(It used to be the style for ladies to wear suspenders, or at least a
good imitation of same which, however, called forth the following lines.)

Sweet girl, I like to see you look
  The very best you can;
But please do not try so soon
  To imitate a man.

You are not masculine or neuter,
  Neither of those genders;
Therefore, I'd advise you to
  Pull off those suspenders.

THY MOTHER'S LOVE.

Thy father will some time reject thee
  When thy path is sin and strife ;
But thy mother will e'er protect thee
  In the thorny paths of life.

Thy sister will some time neglect thee
  When thy face is absent long ;
But thy mother will ne'er forget thee
  In her gentle words of song.

Thy brother will some time detest thee
  When thy feet have gone astray ;
But thy true mother will e'er bless thee
  Till she's laid beneath the clay.

DEPARTED HOPE.

We've seen it fade in youth like the golden rays
    Of yonder setting sun,
From the brightest spot of love in the gentle heart
    Where once it first begun.

We've seen it bid adieu and slowly pass away
    From what it could have blest ;
And have wept as it sunk within the shadowy grave
    In the far distant west.

We've felt its bliss depart from the gentle bosom
    Of peace and perfect love,
Leaving a pain and void until our weary souls
    Are re-united above.

THE BIBLE.

Holy Bible, book sublime,
  Thy promises I believe;
Of a surer balm for mortal wounds
  I can't on earth conceive.

Gracious Word, sweet repose,
  In thy embrace is love;
No surer light can guide my soul
  To yonder's Heaven above.

Opened Word, love eternal,
  No truth thou doth conceal;
This bosom holds no secret thought
  But what thou canst reveal.

Glorious Word, peace divine,
  A cure for every pain;
A searcher of departed lambs—
  Bringing them back again.

Matchless Word, love untold,
  The surest hope of rest;
The smooth tide that bears my soul
  To God's infinite breast.

———

MATTIE.

Mattie, thou knowest I love thee,
  Yet in the weak channels of my mind
  No words sufficient can I find
To express that unfathomable love.

A FALLEN WOMAN.

She has fallen! Oh, God what a pitiful sight
To see one so beautiful, tender and bright,
Fall from the sweet paths of truth and right
Into the lowest slums of sin and night.

Once she was lovely, and pure in her thought;
Kindness and peace in her bosom was wrought;
But now she is stained, even until death
Shall take from her being its last fleeting breath.

Once she was gentle, modest and sweet;
A friendly smile she delighted to greet;
But now she has fallen, her bed is the street,
Her name is too common for men to repeat.

DEATH.

Oh, Death! I tremble at the thought
   Of that cold hand of thine,
That it must blight with iron grasp
   This poor, weak heart of mine.

I tremble that my weary life—
   Tho' 'void of much true worth—
Must ever cease to live again
   In the pleasant paths of earth.

TRUE FRIENDSHIP.

True Friendship! how sweet it is,
   Inadequate are words to tell,
We can but pause in secret thought,
   And ever on its bosom dwell.

TO A DEAR ONE ON THE OTHER SHORE.

Sweet face of thine, departed dead,
Canst thou not linger by my bed
  On this low ground of sorrow,
And bear me a comfort sweet
Till I in heaven thou shalt greet
  On a glorious to-morrow?

I'll look for gentle smiles from thee,
Tho' far beyond life's fitful sea,
  In realms of endless bliss ;
I'll long to view thy shining face
In beauty thro' eternal space,
  Like a sunbeam's sweet kiss.

I'll long to see that lovely face
As it once shone in perfect grace,
  So gentle and divine;
'Twould bear a truer sense of heaven
Than all the gifts God has given
  To this cold heart of mine.

'Twould give me until life is o'er
A firmer hope of that sweet shore
  When Time has passed away ;
'Twould take away my night on earth
And give my soul a sinless birth—
  A grand, transparent day.

———

The winter is here with its dreary winds,
  And chilly nights of snow and frost;
It seems to smile in cold revenge
  On what sweet summer made and lost.

ON THE DEATH OF MR. J. H. W——.

(The highly intelligent gentleman, on whose death this poem is written was a very near and true friend of the author—a native of this city.)

A noble, true man, has passed from the sphere
Of life and its trials, of life and its care,
For the home he longed for, the rest he sought,
He constantly cherished the happiest thought.

He lived but to love, all nature was dear
Unto him whose heart no malice could bear,
And never words from his lips were of strife,
 But love in its fullness composed his life.

'Twas strange that one so noble should die
In the bloom of youth, with a character high;
 Should bid farewell in the noon-tide of life
To two sweet children and a fond, loving wife.

He faded like the rose on a lovely June morn,
To a home and a heaven his spirit was borne;
With a life so pure, so noble and brave,
 He has beautified death and honor'd the grave.

YOURS, NOT MINE.

Years have come and passed away
 Like sunbeams on the sea,
Leaving all their peace in gold
 For YOU and not for me.

Years have come and passed away,
 Their mem'ry brings no sigh,
For rainbows on each zephyr morn
 Adorn'd YOUR eastern sky.

(FIRST VOLUME.)

———

DEDICATED TO MY FRIENDS,

W. H. GIBBES, JR., AND J. WILSON GIBBES,

OF COLUMBIA, S. C.

THE AUTHOR.

TO A FRIEND.

A glance into that face of thine
  Shows friendship sweet ;
A friendship that will never be cast
  Beneath my feet.

I love the impulse of that heart
  Where friendship lives ;
'Tis sweeter to me than the dewy morn
  The spring-tide gives.

I'll praise that noble heart of thine
  Till I pass above ;
'Twill be to me throughout my life
  A source of love.

———

THIS LOCK OF HAIR IN MY WATCH.

After that face is cold and still,
  That face to me so fair,
I'll treasure in a jewel'd case
  This simple lock of hair.

Tho' shadows gather 'round my path,
  Deep sorrow fill the air,
Yet in fond mem'ry I will prize
  This simple lock of hair.

While in that gloomy resting place,
  For which I shall prepare ;
There'll lie within a jewel'd case
  This simple lock of hair.

HER HEART IS MY COTTAGE.

Her heart is my cottage away in the wood,
  And the ivy entwines its door;
Its walls are of love, with entrance ajar
  To welcome the needy and poor.

The lily and violet they cluster around
  The door and all over the lawn,
And no weeds e'er mar their innocent growth,
  For they've long since faded and gone.

I live in this cottage amid the sweet gleam
  Of sunshine and peace on its hearth;
'Tis fairer than the home in which I was born—
  'Tis the happiest spot on earth.

I've rest in this cottage where love is aglow
  As bright as the radiant sun—
I've much to esteem, and naught to regret,
  Since this peaceful life was begun.

Reminiscent of a O'Shanter's best!

ONCE, AND ONLY.

Let us do all the good we can
  While we journey to yonder shore,
For the path we are treading to-day
  We can never tread in any more.

We can never again recall
  The smile on the face that is gone;
We can never make brighter that smile
  We've neglected so long to own.

THE WHITE HEAD'S FAREWELL TO TIME.

"I'll bid thee farewell!" said the frosty head,
  "Farewell to that cold hand of thine;
Long I've been forced to feel thy touch
  On this lone and feeble head of mine."

"Till the noon-day of life my hair was black,
  Parted with care on the left-hand side;
Praised for its brightness and neatness of cut,
  Charming the eyes of the lovers of pride."

"Fair hands have caress'd it many a time
  When life was as fresh as the budding bay;
I lost a few strands as the years rolled by,
  But ne'er once dreamed of its fading away."

"I've fought thee, oh, Time! oft and again,
  Since by the fair fountain of youth I've lain;
I've bathed in its waters, balmy and sweet,
  And never once felt a sorrow or pain."

"But the dew of my life's fond summer is gone,
  Dried up forever by that hand of thine—
I must pass to the grave by thy command,
  Oh, thou eternal, resistless Time!"

———

YOU CRITICS.

Oh, you critics!—if an author errs in a single line,
  That line you'll surely quote,
And will give it as a sample fair
  Of all he ever wrote.

THINK OF ME.

When memory fond shall call you back
  To hours you've spent by the Congaree,
And faces dear and smiles enchanting
  Throng your bosom—think of me.

Think of me on life's dark ocean,
  Toss'd by many a troubled wave;
Bound by fates eternal fetters,
  Floating o'er a gloomy grave.

Think where once your smiles were given
  To cheer me with their bliss untold;
When they were as bright as heaven's,
  Ere your loving words grew cold.

Think when hope was like the morning
  Unclouded, with its peaceful rays;
Where fond anticipation slumber'd
  On its brow in those sweet days.

Think what binds this lonely bosom
  Are the pleasant ties I cannot part—
Constancy in gold and steel
  I trust is graven on your heart.

———

A MOTHER'S LOVE.

There is no love like a mother's love,
  No heart that beats so warm,
No form so delicate that could brave
  Life's battle and its storm.

THE GRAVE OF THE PAST.

As I stand by the weather-beaten grave
    Of the solemn past,
And think of those I might have loved,
    My heart beats fast.

As I think of moments unimproved,
    How strange I feel,
And deep regret into my heart
    Is wont to steal.

I think of the many warning words
    I might have spoken
To comfort that forsaken heart,
    So sadly broken.

I think of the pearl that might have shone
    Lovely and bright,
Now lost in the mould'ring clay
    Of earth's cold night.

While I stand by this neglected grave,
    I feel so lone,
As my heart beats the solemn words,
    The past is gone!

As I stand alone no pleasant sound
    Doth greet my ear,
But the murmuring winds sadly tell
    That all is drear.

No birds sing sweet 'round that lone spot,
    No flowers bloom ;
But ling'ring shadows forever prove
    Its deepest gloom.

Oh, thou Grave! thou dost not hold
    A virtue true ;
Would that I could breathe for thee
    A last adieu !

Would that I from thee forever
    Could turn away,
And make a beautiful, sunny grave
    Of sweet to-day.

NOT TILL THEN.

When I hear thy voice grow harsh,
See thee scan me with contempt,
    And turn thy face away;
Then, not even then, will I
Esteem the love-light in thy heart
    For me a dying ray.

When I feel the grasp of kindness
Slowly turn to a distant touch
    Of thy sweet, gentle hand ;
Then, and not till then, will I
Look on thee as one too strange
    For me to understand.

When I see thee shun my coming,
Pass along some other way,
    Else we should simply meet ;
Then, not even then, will I
Condemn thy being whose sweet face
    I too gladly would greet.

BESIDE THE BROOK.

I take me down beside this babbling brook
With heart made sad by the mem'ry of a look
    From long-loved absent eyes;
I sit me down and learn what I have been
'Mid all the vicissitudes of a life of sin
    In a world of grief and sighs.

I catch a sound—a gentle note of love
From the lonely heart of some sweet mother-dove
    In the distant maple tree;
If she could but speak how gladly she would tell
Of the green hedge where oft she used to dwell
    When her heart was young and free.

Beside this brook where no strange sound is heard
Her young lay sleeping 'neath their parent bird
    On the morn of each summer day;
But some rash hand perhaps from her had borne
Her tender young and left her here alone
    To mourn her sweet life away.

As I list to Nature it seems from yonder sky
I hear a gentler note of music drawing nigh
    Than this from an earthly dove—
'Tis the voice of Annie, whose sweet, plaintive lays
Endear'd me to her in other sunny days
    As she sang to me of love.

My fond Annie, nigh whom I used to dwell
Ere I bade her lovely face farewell,
    And had seen her smiles depart—

BESIDE THE BROOK.

I take me down beside this babbling brook
With heart made sad by the mem'ry of a look
    From long-loved absent eyes;
I sit me down and learn what I have been
'Mid all the vicissitudes of a life of sin
    In a world of grief and sighs.

She loved me in her early days, and too
When her sweet life was ting'd with sorrow's hue
    She loved me still with all her heart.

But she has flown to yonder realms above,
And left me to mourn o'er the mem'ry of that love
    Which she for me has left behind—
Sweet be her rest until we meet again
In that bright world where there's no grief or pain,
    And love's fond ties forever bind.

THE SWEETEST ROSE.

She's too poor to own the costly garments like you possess,
    Or to mingle with your fashionable kind;
Yet you may seek where'er you will in all your giddy circle
    But no such noble heart as hers you'll find.

Her sweet form will ne'er glide like yours o'er the ball-
    room floor
    Two thirds clad in garments rich and fair—
Ah, no, but in the lone chamber where grief and sorrow
    reign
    You'll always find her ministering there.

In your vain eyes she's no better than the servant you em-
    ploy,
    For she was born and reared in obscurity,
Yet 'mid the blended shades and light of this beclouded life,
    She still retained a sweet life of purity.

Know you not that of all the roses that cluster in life's garden,
    No matter how large their petals or how small,
You'll always find the tend'rest and sweetest opening bud
    'Mid the autumn leaves close by the garden wall.

ALICE ON HER BIKE.

I turn me 'round to gaze on thee,
Sweet Alice, with thy gentle eyes,
    And brownish hair,
And looking on thy smiling face,
And slender form of winning grace,
    I call thee fair—

And even true, for truth alone
Dwells in a bosom fair like thine
    Of angel-mould.
My admiration turns to love
As thou, sweet Alice, turtle dove,
    My eyes behold.

I love to view thy slender form
Upon thy bike of shining steel
    Go flying by;
Fain would I start me off and steal
'Round some lone corner where thy wheel
    Might pass me nigh.

———

Few they are, e'en among men of sacret Writ,
That do not ofttimes play the hypocrite—
I have often played it, this I know full well,
But of this my worst of sins I'm not too weak to tell.

———

Tread softly as you roam thro' the garden of life,
    Yea, even on tip-toes,
Or else you may stain with your wayward feet
    The leaves of some sweet rose.

"LET ME LOOSE."

(On the death of two promising boys who were drowned not long since in a river, while attending a Sunday-school pic-nic near this city.)

"Let me loose and I will save you!"
  Cried out a voice young and brave,
As the current dashed them onward
  To a lone and watery grave.

"Let me loose"—but arms grew stronger
  That ere this would save from death—
"And I will save!" but the pleading
  Hushed upon each dying breath.

"Let me loose!" and two fond beings
  Clasped to each other, face to face,
Sunk beneath the gloomy waters,
  Folded in death's cold embrace.

How strange that these two happy boys
  The objects of their mothers' pride,
Should thus be borne in life's sweet morn
  Away from each fond mother's side.

How strange is life!—we know not when
  The hand of death may sever
The ties of love we fain would have
  Bind us on earth forever.

As clasped they were in death's embrace
  While 'neath the waters driven,
So may they to each other's breast
  Be clasped again in Heaven.

BEYOND THE GARDEN WALL.

Down beside a clump of roses,
　　Just beyond the garden wall,
Sat a little brown-eyed maiden
　　Waiting for her beau to call.

It was while the dew was falling
　　Late within the evening hour,
That she sat with careless fingers,
　　Tearing petals from a flower.

"Will he never come," she whisper'd,
　　"I have long been waiting here;
To miss his kisses and caresses
　　Is FAR MORE than I can bear."

"He must know that I adore him,
　　And would linger here till day
If I thought that he was coming,
　　E'en tho' many miles away."

"He is honest and is faithful,
　　And I've often told him so;
But he ne'er has said he loved me,
　　Never answer'd, yes, or no."

"Oh, I hear his footsteps coming,
　　See the light of his cigar;
How it shines within the darkness
　　Like some sweetly glowing star !"

"And I hear him softly humming
　　That lovely little plaintive air
Which he taught me long ago
　　Beside these roses sweet and fair."

"Oh," she whisper'd, "how I love him,
Would his heart I could but gain!"—
And her gentle lips responded
To his own in sweet refrain:—

"What care I for all the roses,
And the violets on the hill,
If the love of my beloved
But lives in my bosom still."

"What care I for all the sunbeams,
And the starlight in the skies,
If I can but see the sunlight
Of his dear, impassion'd eyes."

"What care I tho' other hearts
Often cold, unfaithful be,
So I but know that his true heart
Is ever faithful unto me."

"How patiently I wait to greet him,
In the lonely evening hour,
As I sit beside the roses
Blooming in this lovely bower."

Here she paused, and looking up,
Beheld his fond, familiar face—
"Dear," she said, "come sit beside me
In this lone, secluded place."

And they sat beside the roses
Hand in hand and cheek to cheek;
They never murmur'd or complain'd,
The veil is drawn—let them speak.

POEMS.

THAT GROUP OF SWEET SINGERS.

(On hearing the sweet notes of the singers of the recently organized
choir of the First Presbyterian Church of this city, preparatory to the
reception of a new organ.)

I love to gaze on the fair white forms
   Standing in yon organ loft;
I love to hear their youthful voices
   Gently swelling, sweet and soft.

I love to view their glowing faces
   Fill'd with youth's enchanting smile,
And scent the sweet perfume of roses
   Wafted from their lips the while.

A harp of a thousand golden strings
   Can bear no music half so sweet
As these sad notes that tell my soul
   Of ONE in heaven whom I shall meet.

It seems I hear her once fond voice
   That often whisper'd in these ears—
The mem'ry of her rose-hue'd cheeks
   Brings to these eyes a fount of tears.

Not tears for a young life idly spent
   In the feigned pretence to do the right;
But tears, alas! of grief and pain
   For a disunited heart to-night.

Each note of the sad, sweet music brings
   The mem'ry of other sunny days;
The light of love from gentle azure eyes
   Glows brighter now—celestial rays.

I love the notes that, too, remind me
　Of a brighter home where I shall dwell
When life's strange tide has outward pass'd,
　And I have breathed to earth farewell.

FAREWELL, SWEET ROSE.

(On the death Miss C——, of this city.)

Farewell, sweet budding rose of earth!
　From loved ones thou hast passed away,
O'er death's dark river thou hast sailed
　To await our coming, some sweet day.

Farewell!—but the sound of that sad word
　Soon shall hush on life's cold tide,
We, too, shall pass o'er one by one
　And gather with thee on the other side.

YOU DOMESTIC CRITICS.

Oh, you domestic critics who always quote,
　But cannot e'en compose a readable letter;
I defy you with all your self-blown wisdom,
　To write a decent line of verse—or make mine better.

Fair maid, 'tis a "little gay poem" you wish,
　But you cannot get it to-morrow;
But some sweet day I'll grant your request
　When my heart is free from sorrow.

THAT LITTLE BROWN-EYED LADY.

In a cool and shady cottage
  Beside the rippling Congaree
There's a little brown-eyed lady
  Who is all the world to me.

On her temples blooms the lily,
  From her lips the honey bee
Sips the purest, sweetest nectar.
  Known within this world to me.

On her head the roses cluster,
  On each cheek a crimson hue
Is soften'd by her tender smiles,
  Like rose-tints in morning dew.

In her hand she holds a sceptre
  Like unto a cupid's dart,
And I feel it daily piercing
  Like an arrow in my heart.

O'er her bosom is an armor
  Stronger than the Knight's of old,
'Neath whose surface fits a garment
  Naught but angels can unfold.

'Neath that garment there's a world
  Which no wayward heart can win—
It is by love and love alone
  That I shall ever go therein.

———

Forgive him ere he turns away,
You may need his love another day.

THAT UPPER, WESTERN ROOM.

I hate that upper, western room
  In which a cruel lady sat;
Ah, yes, I feel toward that room
  As the mouse t'ward the hungry cat.

For she whom I can ne'er forgive
  As long as life exists in me,
Oft sat beside that window lone,
  Almost hidden by the elm tree.

I hate that roof all cover'd o'er
  With spring's dead buds and autumn's leaves;
I hate the lonely grave-yard moss
  That clusters 'round its dingy eaves.

I hate that granite window piece
  On which sat a vase of flowers;
I hate the mem'ry of those buds,
  They lost their sweetness in her bowers.

I hate that mirror on the wall
  In which she saw her smiling face;
I hate that powder-puff and paint
  That gave her all her transient grace.

I hate the mem'ry of those hands
  That used to curl that raven hair;
Ah, yes, I hate it, for they moved
  As if no other hands were fair.

I hate that face that never bore
  A single smile to brighten gloom—
Yes, I hate the bitter mem'ry
  Of that upper, western room.

A GREEN ISLE OF REST.

I look away across life's sea
To an eden land prepared for me,
      Of bliss untold ;
My soul longs for that green Isle
As a mother that her absent child
      She might behold.

I look to where I cannot flee—
A green Isle in a heavenly sea,
      A home of rest ;
My soul is wont to launch and float
Unto that Isle, that distant port,
      And leave this breast.

I look to where there's peace in store
And peace can ne'er be parted more
      By Time's cold hand ;
Where all is blessed and serene,
With flowers fresh and grasses green—
      A heavenly land.

I hear sweet music's distant strain,
And it deadens ev'ry sense of pain
      The past has given ;
It almost bears my soul afloat
Into that grand and blessed port—
      My home, my heaven.

———

The human heart like the sensitive plant
  Will close its leaf of love
    If touched by the hand of ingratitude.

SLEEPING 'NEATH THE VIOLETS.

Once on yon lone hill where stands the maple tree
Half-clad with gold and red-tinged autumn leaves,
   My love stood weeping—
Weeping o'er the fickleness of human love—
But now, pillow'd there 'neath the canopy of heaven
   She's gently sleeping.

Little did she think as she gather'd the dewy violets
That in the balmy spring of the approaching year
   She'd be resting there;
That 'mid the maple's shade she always loved so well
The little violets would bloom unseen, unsought,
   And its shade be drear.

She sleeps there alone—as fair as the snow-white robe
That tenderly wrapped her pure and spotless form
   Ere it touched the earth—
Tho' her heart has ceased to beat and her sweet lips are still,
Yet she has bequeathed to mankind all she could :—
   A young life of true worth.

———

"ISN'T THIS BLISS."

O'er against the garden wall, thrice kissed by wayward lips
   She stood pondering and weeping
O'er that momentary bliss known to all fair maidens—
   A stolen kiss.
With ruby lips, bright eyes gazing upward in his face,
   She stood delighted, yet angry;
Till strong arms embraced her, and forgetting all she sighed,
   "Isn't this bliss?"

A REPLY TO A VALENTINE.

The author on receiving a valentine, very prettily gotten up, consisting of a sheet of blue note paper, with ribbon of four colors, red, white, pink and blue, in neat bows fastened in the margin of same, opposite which were appropriate lines in verse, requesting the return of the bows he wished, sent the young lady the following:

My little dear beside the sea,
Quite often I do think of thee—
While o'er this page I sigh and think
A tear falls on this bow of "pink."

My dearest one, then don't repine,
I'll be your loving valentine—
As a token that my love is true,
I'll just return the bow of "blue."

————

Within thy lonely breast, fair one,
    Life's many cares may sorely weigh;
But persevere with faith and love,
    And thou wilt gain thy perfect day.

————

Oh, this transitory life
    With its many, many cares,
Has no balm for mortal wounds
    And no sympathizing tears.

————

All for a transient word of praise
    The poet's days are vainly spent,
Soon his works are all forgotten,
    Yet ingratitude is never meant.

A SWEET OBJECT.

It lay on the back of the bench
  In its magic beauty,
    A jewel rich and fair ;
And as my thoughts enlarged
  How I fondly gazed
    On the sweet thing lying there.

It lay on the back of the bench,
  A mysterious object
    I could not understand ;
Yet I loved its angel-shape,
  As my passionate gaze
    Sunk to her matchless hand.

ENDURANCE.

Every sunbeam has its shadow,
Every shadow has its sorrow,
  Sorrow that we all must bear ;
Thro' that shadow and that sorrow
Hope renew'd will bear us onward
  To a home more bright and fair.

A SNOW COVERED EARTH.

Would I were a star in the heavens,
  Conscious and having being,
That I might peep between the parting clouds
  On nature's grand attire—
    A snow-cover'd earth.

TO FAIR NINA.

Fair Nina, your fondest girlhood years
Have been like youth's enchanting dream,
    Careless and sweet;
Around your path each sunny hour
Roses have budded and violets bloom'd
    Beneath your feet.

Many bright suns have shown within
That dewy path which your fond feet
    Did then pursue;
'Twas in those sweet and happy hours
You gather'd in your peaceful heart
    Character true.

Many have sought and often loved
Your snowy hand, but all in vain—
    You dreamed of me,
And I of you—tho' we've never met—
Those dreams may have a meaning, tho'
    We're both at sea.

––––––

The sweetest rose of life may it ever entwine
The warm-beating heart in that bosom of thine,
And the lilac that bloom'd in my childhood's hour,
May it ever make fragrant thy loneliest bower.

––––––

Thou art fairer to me than all I perceive
From the dawn of the morn till the close of the eve,
And when the clouds have veiled fair lunar's bright light,
Still thou art to my heart a perfect delight.

TO DORA.

I wonder, as my memory calls
  Me back to other sunny days,
If she e'er thinks of him who still
  Adores all her winning ways.

Her dark brown eyes, so pure, sublime,
  With soft and peaceful glow;
Fain would I live in that lone spark
  That's burning sweet and low.

Not burning low as a dying spark
  Within a tear-stain'd, dying eye,
But a holy gleam of gentle love,
  As clear as the noon-day sky.

I wonder, tho' she is far away,
  If she ever thinks of me,
And the glances we've exchanged
  While beside the Congaree.

Oh, sacred eyes, if e'er you gaze
  On these lone words of mine,
Look up, and think of him whose love
  Is traced in every line.

A WISH.

'Round thy path may roses cluster,
  And o'er thy head the myrtle twine,
And ne'er a ray of hope grow dim
  Within that gentle heart of thine.

TO FLORENCE, LILY AND NONIE.

My fond sisters, and can I close this feeble work
    Which tho', perhaps, unknown to fame may be,
Without here inscribing from my inmost heart
    That ardent love I've always borne for thee.

When other forms that feigned to stand beside me
    Left me to drift alone on life's cold tide ;
Thy dear forms with outstretch'd arms received me,
    And passed adown life's journey by my side.

Tho' earth's dark clouds may gather 'round my heart,
    And the star of hope grow dim upon its shrine,
Yet 'mid the shadows that then would sink within me,
    I'd find sweet rest in that true love of thine.

————

A WISH.

On the sunny side of life I trust
    To see your gentle footsteps wend,
And in those loving words "well done"
    May your peaceful journey end.